Astara (Tatiana Aster) is an international certified personal consultant, trainer of original group programs with 25 years of experience, Doctor of Naturopathy, author of the books *Seven Facets of Reality. Awakening. Creation. Success* and *The Astara Effect.* Specialization in counselling is the maximum realization of a person's mental, intellectual, physical, and social potential. She is a certified trainer with an audience of more than 2,500 clients in the cities of Germany, the USA, Italy, Spain, Japan, the Czech Republic, and the CIS on three grants from private and government foundations for research in the field of psychology of influence. She holds more than 100 certificates of completion of specialized seminars and additional educational courses and is the founder of the public organization Aster Evolution, which unites more than 200 masters in the field of consciousness development around the world. The ideological inspirer and organizer of more than 35 cultural and educational expeditions to the countries of Europe, Asia, and the CIS, she is also the author of the healing method of restoring the biorhythmic settings of the body, Astroyoga.

Find more information about Astara on the web:
https://tatianaaster.de/

Astara

LOVE AND
(OR, NOT) INTIMACY

AUSTIN MACAULEY PUBLISHERS®

LONDON • CAMBRIDGE • NEW YORK • SHARJAH

A CIP catalogue record for this title is available from the British Library.

ISBN 9781035841776 (Paperback)
ISBN 9781035841783 (Hardback)
ISBN 9781035841790 (ePub e-book)

www.austinmacauley.com

First Published 2025
Austin Macauley Publishers Ltd®
1 Canada Square
Canary Wharf
London
E14 5AA

Table of Contents

There was once a king who had three daughters. The youngest, named Psyche, was so beautiful, that no one could compare and people began to worship her.

This enraged the goddess Venus. She ordered her son, Cupid, to make Psyche fall in love with the most unattractive man and suffer from unrequited love all her life.

Cupid went to carry out his mother's order, but when he saw Psyche, he himself fell madly in love with her and wanted Psyche to become his wife.

One day, the wind picked her up and carried her to a beautiful palace of gold, ivory, and gems. Psyche entered the palace, and someone unseen whispered: "From now on you are my wife. Fear nothing and reign here. Soon I will come to you."

Psyche began to live in this palace. She spent the day alone, and only at night, in complete darkness, did her mysterious husband come to her. He was gentle and kind, swore his endless love to her, but often said that if one day she saw his face, he would leave her forever.

One day, Psyche could not endure the unknown. As her husband fell asleep, she lit an oil lamp and moved closer to see his appearance. Seeing how handsome Cupid was, she laughed with joy. Her hand trembled, and a few drops of hot oil fell on Cupid's shoulder. He immediately woke up and, without a word, flew away.

Psyche lay on the ground and wept bitterly. Realising that Cupid would never return to her, she got up and went in search of him.

At last, Psyche appeared before Venus. The goddess bulked millet, poppy seeds, lentils, and beans into one pile and ordered the girl to sort them and put all the grains separately. Anant with its friends helped her, and quickly got the job done.

The next time Venus ordered her to bring a piece of golden wool from the sheep that were grazing across the river. The reeds growing by the river advised her to simply gather all the golden wool that the sheep leave on the branches of the bushes.

Then Venus demanded that Psyche fill up a jug with icy water from a high mountain spring. And an enormous eagle helped her with that.

Finally, the angry Venus gave Psyche a box and told her to go down to Hades and ask Persephone for a blush.

But Psyche managed to complete this task, too, thanks to the advice of the stone tower, which spoke to her in a human voice. But curiosity took the best of her, and she opened the box. The eternal dream immediately flew out of it and Psyche, as if dead, fell to the grass.

Meanwhile, Cupid sought his beloved, gathered the eternal dream from her eyelids, put it back into the box, and with a prick of his arrow woke Psyche up.

Cupid flew to Olympus and begged Zeus, his father, to help him. Zeus agreed and presented Psyche with a goblet of nectar; after drinking it, she became immortal. After that, Cupid and Psyche lived happily ever after and were never separated again.

This book is a journey into Wonderland. Wonders that are scattered all around us and have gone unnoticed. Wonders that we can only guess and don't even know about. It turns out that the real wonder can be ourselves and our relationships with those whom we love and hate, whom we are trying to catch and from whom we run for our life.

This is a book about dreams becoming reality. About how to achieve happiness in love and intimacy in this life and in all the coming ones. The author shares with the reader the innermost secrets drawn from a variety of sources of wisdom and secret knowledge, as well as from the experience of her own amazing life.

Those who don't feel,
That it is Love that attracts them,
Like a river;
Those who do not drink the dawn,
Like a cup of spring water;
Who do not taste the sunset,
Like an evening meal;
Those who do not wish to change,
Let them sleep.
This Love is above the teachings of the theologians,
These old tricks and hypocrisies.
If thou hopest in this way
To refine the mind
Go back to sleep.
I have abandoned my reason,
I've torn all my clothes to shreds
And threw them away
If you're not naked
Wrap yourself in a fine
Cloak yourself in words
And sleep.
Rumi Jalal ad-Din Muhammad Balkhi

From the Author

My path to feeling love consciously has been through a huge amount of illusions, unrealised needs, and infantile expectations. Love was waiting for me on a very different shore, very far from the point from which I began to build my first relationship.

I saw a huge number of people who had not yet reached love in their minds and hearts. And even more of those who will never get to it because they are stuck at one of the turning points. There are many similar stories unfolding all over the world.

The relationship between a woman and a man leaves no one indifferent and permeates our entire being. It affects everything, and everything affects it. This crucial segment of our lives contains so many problems and questions that sometimes we don't know what to grasp at.

Could it be that relationships are predetermined by our karma and we can't influence anything? Or are they conditioned by our family histories and we have to study genealogy, work with family energy, do alignments? Or everything depends on our personality and you have to work on yourself or with a psychologist? Or everything is determined by our success in society, and it makes sense to get wealth, status, and spectacular appearance?

Or should we just start an active search, making all the acquaintances and arranging dates, and then a suitable partner will definitely be found? Or should we just pray to God and wait for him to send us the right person? Or should we not wait, but make lists of desirable qualities and visualise the image of the ideal partner? Or should we collect all the horoscopes, calculate compatibility, and take the search for a partner into our own hands?

Or is it better not to strive for a partnership at all, but to develop the Anima and the Animus[1], leading them to an inner marriage?

Truth probably includes all of the above to one degree or another.

This book will not answer all the questions about gender relations, but it can be a reference or a guiding star, with which you will follow a path that is sure to lead you to a more harmonious and happier loving relationship. And, whoever that relationship is with, whatever form it takes, ultimately it will be your relationship with yourself and with God, which is the same thing.

---

1 Anima and Animus are terms introduced into psychology by C. Jung to refer to the archetypes associated, respectively, with the female and male gender.

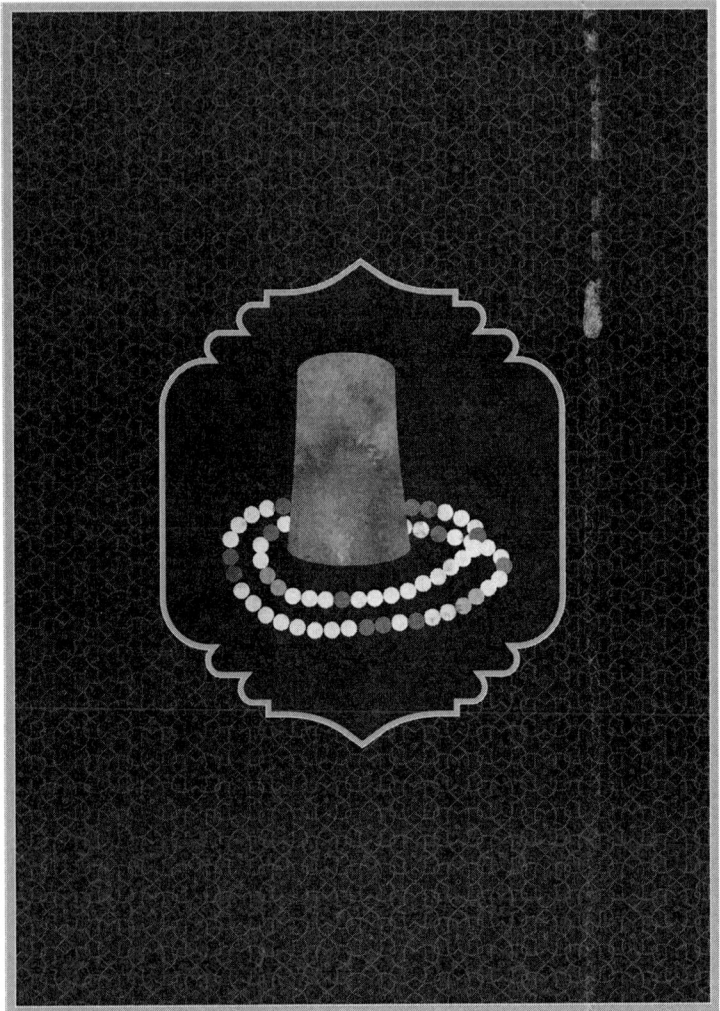

Part I
Love Classified as 'For Personal Use Only'

The Diamond Facets of Love

So many believe that love is the saving apotheosis of mercy, the antithesis of hostility and hatred. That love heals and comforts, that it is the answer to one's deepest dreams and prayers for serenity, beauty, and pleasure. However, the more one strives for this magic, the more effort one puts into one's own love play, the deeper one sinks into despair.

Despair at the inescapable vulgarity, at the loneliness and the futility of all attempts to build the very ideal relationships, lasting and beautiful. With each step towards apparent happiness, dreams recede and melt away like a mirage. The mirage is replaced by old age, with its consolation of intimacy and humility with fate.

Most people leave this world with a completely lonely, broken, and cold heart in their chests, one that has experienced much but never found what everyone is looking for: coveted love.

Love, by its very nature, has nothing to do with stable promises and parental security. Yes, a family cannot exist without these principles, but they also kill love. As soon as a person reaches stability and security, they begin to destroy their world out of boredom. And then their road is certainly not love, but war itself.

The nature of love is so deep and mysterious that any attempt to force it into the concrete experience of one's life always ends in failure. On the contrary, the mysteries of love, realised and passed through the soul, opens doors to another world where love, freedom, self-realisation and power become the natural foundation of all our lives.

The importance of the relationship between a man and a woman cannot be overestimated. Humanity owes its birth to them. People of the opposite sex surprise us, attract us, interest us, sometimes break our heart, but we are ready to dive into the whirlpool of love again and again. Man and woman, like two tongues of flame, swirl around each other, diverging and reconnecting.

If we look at the relationship in terms of trinitarianism, we will see its presence in all three spheres.

In a clan, in a family, the couple is what forms both the family and the clan and ensures its continuation. Even in same-sex couples, there is usually a certain balance of feminine and masculine roles and manifestations.

In our personal psychological space, which can be referred to the lower world, interest in the opposite sex is also extremely important.

Oedipus and Elektra[2] complexes, which have a huge impact on our whole life and which we experience at about

---

2 Oedipus complex is a term used by Sigmund Freud in his theory of psychosexual development to describe the feelings of a boy who desires his mother and feels jealousy and anger towards his father. The Electra Complex is a psychoanalytic term introduced by Carl Jung in 1913 describing a girl's desire to compete with her mother for her father's love.

the age of three, are tied to the quality of the masculine-feminine relationship between parents. In addition, there are inner figures in each of us, not only of a child, an adult and a parent, but also of a woman and a man—they are called in some traditions Anima and Animus, or described as the marriage of the inner king and queen.

In society, women and men try to attract each other, sometimes even engaging in gender competition. Men are responsible for the external boundaries, representing the couple in society, while women give men the energy to be active in it. It is sometimes jokingly said that without women, men would not build houses, palaces and roads, they would not care about their status and appearance, but would be satisfied with little and be perfectly content.

Patriarchy affects not only the generic fields, but it also affects the entire material world. Men by nature are more active, aiming at development, expansion, and capture, whereas women's nature suggests qualities of preservation, saving, caring, patience, and passivity.

And perhaps with a more balanced distribution and cooperation of male and female energies in the world of society, we would live on a healthier and more love-filled planet Earth, with fewer wars and natural disasters.

Speaking of the third world, the spiritual one, we can think of the idea of 'one's soulmate', without whom we seem unable to achieve true happiness and bliss and which we are always searching for. Yin (feminine) and Yang (masculine) are also concepts from the spiritual world. In most of the world's religions, there is no balance of feminine and masculine.

Woman is present more often in the image of a mother, although in fact the female ability to generate new worlds, to build them in cooperation with male energy, makes men and women equal partners-creators.

Love is work, and falling in love is a primary loan.

Falling in love lasts for three years. The rose and candy stage or passion passes even faster. Usually, the more time people spend together (and get used to each other, transferring to the stable category of 'sweethearts') the faster it is. As a rule, this is enough for gender programs or the process of reproduction—marriage, birth of children—to take place.

It turns out that this is a kind of a loan, and after spending it, it is necessary to make your own efforts to consciously build a relationship. Instincts take part in the loan of falling in love.

Love is a choice. But it is not a passive choice where something happens to us and we choose to take it for granted. Every day we have to make a conscious decision to love our partner.

People think of love as a fun, a pleasant emotion, but it is, in fact, pretty hard work, labour. Like all work, there are many pleasurable moments, but it does not cease to be work.

Women and men have different roles.

Much has been written about the differences between them. And women are incredibly different from each other, and the same goes for men. Understanding these differences makes life considerably easier, as does getting rid of any ignorance.

In a couple, the woman is responsible for the microclimate, the happiness in the family, that is, for the internal boundaries, and the man for the external ones.

Shishkov[3] has an example: the man gives the house, and the woman fills it with dowry and makes this house a home.

In terms of energy, there are also many differences. A woman is grounded by nature, while a man is energised by the Cosmos. So maybe women are consciously trying to be more spiritual and graceful, while men are practical.

Yin and Yang are essentially Woman and Man—two dualities. Either extreme is bad, like a tyrant woman or a slacker man. Those we admire have both dualities developed and balanced. For example, it is a beautiful, intelligent, feminine lady with a strong character (there are enough examples of this in movies, and the sphere of basic realisation can be completely different—gender, society, or spirituality—or a combination of them).

Or it is a strong charming and charismatic man, creative and successful, who is in rapport with his feelings and emotions.

We know different archetypes of femininity and masculinity. For example, there is the Greek pantheon of gods. There are also the archetypes of the inner king and queen, and they are always paired.

---

3 S. N. Shishkov is a psychologist, writer and philosopher. He is the author of the psychological concepts 'Ring of Perception', 'Seven-year cycles of personality development: age crises', 'Structure of the unconscious: Tornado of consciousness', 'Typology: 12 personality types', 'The way of the hero: the myth of social realisation'. Author of *Stalking: the Art of Interaction*; *From Boy to Sage. Men's Secrets*; *The Ordinary Miracle or the Key to the Unconscious*.

There are many kinds of love. People use this word for feelings for pets, for children and grandchildren, for parents, brothers and sisters, for friends, for a partner, for God.

There is unconditional and conditional love. Unconditional love is only possible on a divine level. Love for children resembles unconditional love, but instincts are mixed in with it.

There is, in fact, no generally accepted definition of 'true love'. People apply the definition to everything from sexual desire and co-dependent relationships to an adoration for croissants and a passion for sports cars. Probably all sensations connected in one way or another with the production of endorphins are commonly referred to as love. A special status is assigned to only one additional concept— falling in love, characterised by a brief fireworks of intoxicating emotions and the predominance of pink tones in the interior.

For other types of love, no words have been found yet, because everyone falls in love, but how to name and research what happens later (few people come to these stages of love)? Don't dig in the literature and don't torture your fellows with questions—no one knows anything about it. Simply, when people experience particularly pleasant feelings in someone else's company, they habitually call it love, and when those incredible feelings fade away, they say that love is gone.

Interestingly, all kinds of deviance are also love, only perverted. Religious fanatics supposedly love God (but only themselves in God, not the other way around). Rapists love forced sex. Gluttons love to fill their bellies. Tyrants love power, harpagons love money, and 'workaholics' to sweat their guts out, no matter what.

Love manifests itself on the level of personality, personal relationships, lineage, and family (in the 'lower world').

Socionics asserts that true happiness is only possible in a dual relationship. It turns out that one is a puzzle for one's dual. Of course, not every dual will be super-loving. But if there are other factors—attraction, shared values, social compatibility—duality becomes a great compliment.

When a relationship is not dual, there is inevitably tension, false hopes, disappointment, misunderstanding, arguments and quarrels. And duality generates a state of a certain magical comfort. For the same manifestation of yours your antipode will curse you, and the dual will praise.

Relationships in a couple to a degrees are also affected by the gender norms. Generally, conflicts arise when there is no compliance with the norms developed through society or family values. In addition, people are in a family system, which has its own goals, and this aspect is necessarily taken into account.

Love manifests itself at the level of society (in the 'middle world'), and society also strongly influences the relationship.

Love on the level of spirituality (in the 'upper world') is possible when people are spiritualised and build relationships, understanding that the partner is not just a person, but a creature with a soul and a spirit, with their own and society's evolutionary relationships.

Love is the driving force behind human evolution. People are often bound together by karmic relationships, various predestinations and evolutionary tasks due to the couple's relationship, all of which are very important parts of the overall evolution of humanity.

Alone you can develop spiritually faster, but you can go further as a couple.

Shishkov, in his course on the cycles of life, gives the paired relationship a very important foundation upon which everything is built. This does not mean that people without children or without a couple do not develop, but their development is somewhat different.

Shishkov proves in both the men's and women's courses that the father and the mother figures strongly influence the formation of personality. And this is reflected not only in a person's gender project, but in their whole life. For example, you can compare the path of a bitch and the path of a blue stocking—these are really different life paths, and it all starts with the figures of 'M' and 'F' in childhood.

We are in a perpetual search for our soulmate, and in fact, we can't get away from it on Earth until other races without gender division emerge. Still, it is worth considering an inner marriage, in which a soulmate can be found and developed within oneself. But it is much more fun and enjoyable to live with a soulmate in a marriage harmoniously manifested in all three worlds than alone or with a mate or relatives.

The importance of this for evolution cannot be overstated. People at all times are constantly thinking about money, power, and love. Of course, the advanced ones also think about creativity and service, about truth and knowledge.

Only no one can miss love.

Love is given to us as a tool of evolution. And evolution is the knowledge of all aspects of God and the pursuit of the union with Him. This incredible supreme substance defines all of our lives and becomes the main driving force of evolution. God is love, and everything flows out of love. And we create because we love the fruits of our labour.

Love and Ego.

A human is made up of personality—the ego—such invasive structures that crave resources, desire better and pleasant things for themselves. And, at the same time, one has the opposite, divine qualities—altruism and service, unselfishness and self-giving, self-sacrifice and acceptance. In a relationship, everything is usually mixed up, and it is difficult to separate one from the other, to reconcile these parts in yourself and in your partner.

And the level of maturity and immaturity of partners is also very important. Children are more selfish and parents are more altruistic.

Love and sex.

Love in a couple has to do with sex. Tantra can be anything. And from love, children are born.

Love and Needs.

Our needs are a technical assignment to the universe. The better we become aware of our needs and differentiate them by sorting out what we have inherited from our lineage and family, by separating our desires from social gender stereotypes, and by learning to realise and recognise our deeper needs, the better grip of the assignment we are broadcasting we have.

By knowing our desires, healing and compensating for unhealthy or overdue needs, we directly affect our lives, including the realm of relationships and love.

So, love is an extraordinary phenomenon that has an infinite number of hypostases, definitions, facets, and peculiarities. It is impossible to understand what it is in its entirety by looking at it from a single point. Love is multidimensional, like the universe itself. Love is a flow moving through the labyrinth of divine Providence.

It is possible to understand and comprehend the essence of this flow only by diving into it. And its source is in receiving the initiation of independence, adulthood, separation, and in gaining one's own resources to 'pay for love'.

The Final Withdrawal from the Parental Home in One's Own Mental and Psychological World

The Essence of Child Attachment.

It is no secret that children do not have love as such, they only have attachment. Their lives depend on the successful realisation of it.

A child's emotional habit to attachment in traditional ancient communities was corrected during puberty with the help of special rituals and practices. It was extremely important to detach the adolescent from the object of attachment and give them emotional freedom. The rituals included various radical practices that both boys and girls had to undergo.

If a teenager is not led through the ritual of breaking attachment to everything and everyone that was valuable to them as a child, they will become co-dependent in adulthood. There is an opinion that co-dependence does not occur if a child had a perfectly happy childhood, if their parents gave them the entirety of intimacy.

In other words, modern concepts of psychology argue that co-dependency is the result of the child's unmet (in an ecological form) basic needs for various forms of intimacy. But the experience of ancient civilisations tells us that the child has no limit to the absorption of attention and care, and them themselves are not able to leave their attachments.

They can only be ritually cut off so that they give way to absolute emotional freedom, which is then, thanks to adult motives and individual values, is realised in the love, friendship and belonging of an adult, self-sufficient person.

It is important to understand that our childpart is capable solely of merging, total connection, the ecstasy of unity, and absolute emotional control. We do not perceive our attachment carriers as subjects; we recognise them as objects, thereby depriving them of their free will. This functioning of the child part harmonises with adult life only in the most subtle and sensual moments: during sex or emotional intimate contact between two people, during prayer, and so on.

That said, if access to child ecstatic merging is blocked, we will need special help to heal our orgasms and the erotic script of life in general.

So, the childlike ability to merge with someone or something in ecstasy is something we need in bed, in the kitchen, in creativity—be it writing, drawing or dancing. In short, our childlike spontaneity and ecstasy are needed wherever simplicity, ease, openness, purity, and another person's ingress into our soul, energy, state, or penetration between partners' bodies is required.

The three pillars upon which all ingress is based are trust, security, and motivation. Children's motivation is curiosity and the desire to develop. And trust and safety arise where there is clear, consistent contact that helps us discover our nature and individuality without pressure, stress or aggression. When our child part feels trust, safety and motivation to be creative, motivated to play, we go in for rapprochement.

But how sad it is if one does not break the habit of their childhood attachment in time, during adolescence. Basically, they will never know true love. Because to all positive stimuli (trust, security and motivation) they will only respond through childhood attachment (merging, unity, complete emotional control), which means that their feelings, mind, emotions, and decisions will not be free to fulfil adult strategic personality interests.

If one wants true love, one must first learn not to become attached or bound. You have to take a step back, look inside yourself and analyse whether everything was okay with your teenage sexuality and what is left to be done to teach your inner teenager total, self-directed freedom. Of great value on earth is the love of those people who have been able to love by being free, having overcome the egocentrism of childhood possession of an object.

An adult person without childhood attachments cultivates the service to love by the power of their spirit as the supreme need for self-expression and for the self-actualisation of the desire to give to another person part of their strength, possibilities, and energy. Mature love is born because we see our partner not as an object but as a subject, a whole world revealed to us in the beauty of our service to this world as a part of God.

In ordinary life, when a person feels the touch of love for another through the impulse of their spirit, they begin to struggle with their inner unseparated teenager, who very much wants stability, emotional power, the use of their partner's feelings for their own benefit, which invariably causes pain to the object of such 'love'. Third parties may also be involved in this kind of relationship and contribute to the intimacy war.

The unseparated person often hesitates to ask important questions of his or her partner because he or she is afraid of rejection, afraid of being rejected. For our inner child, rejection is really tantamount to death, for he or she is aiming for a full merger. An adult, on the other hand, can, and should, insist on transparent forms of agreement, on attachments that are predictable and understandable to both parties.

Exercise

The answers to these questions help us learn about the structure of children's sensuality embedded in our consciousness and subconscious at a very early age.

1. What childhood attachments are extremely important to you in life and relationships?
2. What defence mechanisms have you built around your attachments, and what do you pay to keep those mechanisms running?
3. What do you rely on most in your attachments?
4. What fears do you have about your attachments?
5. What are you willing to do to get what or who you feel attached to?
6. What are you really losing in your adult life as you guard your attachment dreams?
7. What interesting, adult, grandiose tasks are you not accomplishing because your time is spent frustrating

and controlling the objects of attachment because they don't satisfy your hopes and dreams?

8. What is the ultimate reward of attachment for you?

It's important to understand that childhood attachments themselves only tend to increase, supersede everything else over time, including our adult ambitions, discovering talents, and being able to love through emotional freedom. These days, attachments in the consumption structure are growing by leaps and bounds.

Just look at the ever-expanding markets for services and material goods whose production is destroying the planet, all based on an unquenchable childhood thirst for the experience of attachment. This can be attachment to objects and things, receiving emotions and feelings from them, forming relationships on the level of possession.

Infantile civilisation arises precisely because the law of the mental transition of the child or adolescent into an adult, a responsible person with a strategic consciousness is broken.

The issue of initiation for adulthood is not solved at the level of social institutions because it is too closely connected with the sacred sphere, with the human soul, with its blood, with the memory of ancestors. Besides, the exit from the territory of childhood attachment is not into the structure of society, but into the structure of one's own spirit.

Subsequently, a person may, of course, achieve social results, but growing up itself is a deeply individual process. Abandoning one's own childhood attachments is a process so painful and merciless mentally that only the rigid conditions of the ritual can overcome the resistance one experiences upon entering the path of initiation.

The importance of finding one's place in adolescence.

An adolescent who has successfully undergone the initiation of ridding themselves of childhood attachment to the care of their parents experiences an unimaginable, incomparable thirst for adventure, freedom, knowledge of the world and their own abilities. They must go through this wild period precisely in order to learn to deal with all the resources of the world—the resources of communication, friendship, enjoyment, creativity, learning, and recognition.

The most important thing they need to experience is a sense of their own place in the world, without which further freedom as an adult would make no sense.

Finding a place in the world begins with gaining recognition of one's sexual status among other adolescents. It is the attitude of peers that determines an adolescent's sexuality—his or her awareness of the value of his or her sexuality and the ability to deal with it. Thus, the chances of successfully forming a relationship and a couple in adulthood are determined not only by the amount of love and care received from parents.

The success of your love life depends largely on whether other boys and girls have recognised your attractiveness and what place they have given you in the attractiveness ranking. Those who couldn't get their place may be stuck in this phase for a long time, and will spend their lives changing partners, creating competition in their personal lives for other people.

Competitive behaviour in personal relationships is one of two things.

Either it is a sign of objective scarcity (which is very rare these days, since we live in an overpopulated world and have an overabundance of attention and communication).

Or it is a sign of a total lack of connection with the resource within us (a subtle trust is broken, and there is no feeling that we are connected with the resource of pleasure in one relationship firmly, comfortably, and securely).

Through experimentation, trial and adventure, the adolescent learns this world and takes from it their own, what really matters to them. In this situation, they are independent, create their own style of exchange with the world, are focused on the expression of individuality, and are devoid of anxiety about the future, because they believe in their own strength.

This state is incredibly appealing and gives access to the inner charisma of holding on to one's life status.

Exercise

To see if you are ready in your sexuality to transition from adolescence to adulthood, try answering the following questions.

1. What impression do I make on partners of the opposite sex as a person to desire?
2. Do I desire myself, and in what way? Am I attractive to myself in my own world?
3. Am I able to sublimate my instincts and strong feelings into creativity and other, socially acceptable forms of expression?
4. Do I have my own style?
5. Can I give myself what I want on my own?

6. Can I control my own level of anxiety in matters important to me?
7. How do I develop my art of sharing things and feelings that are valuable to me with other people?

Many disorders are now considered a condition that reaches the level of clinical. Narcissists, neurotics, and unstable personalities seem to swarm around us, according to the classifications. But the percentage of actual clinical manifestations is not that high. Far more are those who simply failed in their adolescence to establish a healthy ego—socially, sexually, creatively and spiritually.

Not being rooted in the needs of our inner teenager is what determines behaviour that is very similar to borderline clinical one (the person is simply unable to take and give away the values they want in a comfortable way). People who are psychologically in the adolescent phase are always fighting for something—for love, for a place, for respect, for resources.

Only an adult can build and multiply, and they do not need to fight because they are capable of taking and creating everything they need.

Teenage infatuation is the most destructive feeling in the world because it is filled with the energy of jealousy, passion, and control multiplied by the volcanic force of psychological puberty. The nuclear attraction of falling in love in unseparated adolescents is sometimes prescribed as the only pattern of emotional behaviour in adults if, as teenagers, they were absorbed in forming their sexual instinct and self-pleasure instead of socialising and gaining distance and freedom from the family.

Later on, this pattern of behaviour is formed as the only correct one under conditions of increasing sex hormones, and it is very, very difficult to go beyond it even through conscious activity.

The Hard Separation
Scenario in Relationships

If all of the above has not helped you come to a healthy separation in a relationship, then there is one last remedy: to accept and finally realise that your lover is and always has been a stranger to you and, moreover, should remain so in the future.

Adam and Eve as basic archetypes were not originally sister and brother to each other in spirit. Kinship itself kills the opposing potentials, and thus the power of mutual attraction. We are genuinely attracted only to those who are not like us and, at the same time, are not opposed to us.

With a stranger, our paradigm of behaviour and thinking changes dramatically: it turns out that they owe us nothing beyond what we have agreed upon and what they want to give us.

A person who clings strongly and hopelessly to a husband or wife, a friend or a girlfriend, receives a sobering blow when they realises their genetic non-kinship with their partner. There is no place for playing roles of father and mother, brothers and sisters, the close blood circle of kinship. Recognition of the partner as a stranger on the physical level gets rid of illusory kinship and forces one to work harder on becoming truly related to each other on the level of the soul.

I had a case in my practice where a man brought his wife to a class; at the time they were on the verge of divorce. They hung on each other emotionally, mutually exhausted by expectations of understanding, support, and help. Of course, each felt that the other was not giving them enough of it. Both were from functional, full families, and carried the format of functional merger into their new family.

They had a young child, and the situation was threatening to become a disaster. I suggested that they admit that they were complete strangers to each other and stay in this new psychological status for at least a week. I can say that now they live very happily because each of them has taken on their own amount of work to build true intimacy against accepting the fact of initial disconnection.

This technique of acknowledging each other as strangers also helps when a couple's sexual relationship has ended. Between people who have become morally related to each other and in light of this began to get along well, sex always goes into oblivion. Because they begin to feel blood kinship, even though it is an illusion.

And even if on the physical level sex between them remains, on the creative, emotional level, their flirting will fade away very quickly, they will stop 'turning on' each other.

The ancient rituals of separating a teenager made them 'dead' to their own family, and only after that a boy or girl was considered ready for sexual relations, in which no one restricted them anymore.

In a healthy relationship between two separated partners, each seeks solace in the strength of their own spirit and soul, seeks the power of practice and the building up of one's own potential. No one uses the other as a crutch. In the highest sense, man and woman give each other the quintessential masculinity and femininity.

They are independent, have brightness, charisma, and inspiration. Such a partner one wants to be romantic with all their life, increasingly attracted to them by their strengths, captivating them by their attractiveness.

The sexual life of people living in true love does not end until death. And most people artificially suffocate it themselves, making each other first a father and a mother, who must accept and understand everything, support, comfort and warm, and then becoming grandparents for each other. Here, of course, it will be difficult to withstand the heat of sexual passion because a relative must be protected, not charmed.

By the way, charming is a more developed mental function, and it belongs to higher capacities of our brain than feeling warmth of a blood relative.

Modern people are stressed by the development of civilisation. But, instead of accepting the challenge and becoming stronger, they become more infantile and dim in sex and in love. The whole scenario of flirting, playing, seducing, charming lasts, at most, six months (usually premarital), and culminates in marriage.

And after the wedding, a long period of breaking and remaking each other in order to get a second family in the form of mom and dad. Because their child parts are involved in this process, the partners often blackmail each other with the wounds and trauma of their inner children. In the end, they either break down and adjust or break up.

If the author of this book is wrong, and there is a third option, show me such a wife and a husband whose art of flirting, seduction, play, and attraction has become even more perfect after ten years of marriage. Did this couple reach a truly tantric level of pleasure, learning all the deep secrets of each other's orgasms? Did their love connect their spiritual and physical spaces, giving them a sense of god and goddess presence in their relationship?

Show such a couple and the author will eat her hat.

Our society has stopped producing such couples because it requires the love of two adults who are healthy, independent, and self-sufficient on all levels. Individuals with powerful creative potential, which they do not seek from their partner, sucking it up to the last drop, but, on the contrary, bring it into the relationship themselves as their own finished product of soul and personality.

The Problems of Unseparated Couples.

The problem with an unseparated partner is not that sooner or later you will be disappointed in their social and financial abilities. Nor is it that they will turn out to be not the most effective parent. It's not that they will grow old very ugly and will be very disappointed in themselves. And it's not even that the resources of sensations and energy in your couple will be constantly lacking.

The main problem is that such a partner will methodically follow the instructions of their inner child, who is horrified by how different you are from the way their mother and father were in the first year of their life. This inner child has very precise subconscious instructions in all areas: what and how you should do things, how to live, how to give intimacy, spend money, have sex and behave in public.

And this child, under the guise of sexual instincts and supposedly adult relationships, will produce a subtle mutation of your underlying nature of individuality. At the same time the partner themselves are also under the spell and hypnosis, under the blackmail of their child, and deeply convinced that all their requests have deep, correct and rational grounds and meanings.

Here are some examples of the attitudes of unseparated husbands:

- The order in the house should be determined by me, because you are not capable to manage it yourself;
- I manage all the finances better than you do, and I will control it;
- you should be on my mother's side, to understand and accept her position;
- my children from previous marriages will always come first for me;
- my first wife is my closed one, my relative, and she will always be present in my life;
- you must not have a counsellor or any other contacts I am not aware of;
- I don't have to consider your opinion.

Such attitudes look like symptoms of narcissism, but they are not always behind a clinical disorder. The same signs are present when the inner child takes over the partner's subconscious and wants a second mother or a second father at the expense of their couple's relationship.

Examples of the attitudes of unseparated wives:

- you must always remember that I can't protect myself;
- you took me from my family and therefore, you are responsible for me now;
- you are to blame for our family's problems;
- you must always be stronger than me;
- our relationship is more important than your self-realisation;
- you must serve my inner princess;
- you must always be responsive;
- you have to learn to belong to your family.

No one can handle child aggression in marriage when it comes to infantile partners. You can't just take and stop it in yourself, and you can't stop it in a spouse. Unfortunately, remaking each other into mom/dad shuts down the higher potential for development and leads to deep emotional dysfunction.

If you were in such a relationship and got divorced, don't feel bad. You should understand that a divorce in such a situation means that you had adult parts that saved your psyche from further destruction. It doesn't matter if it was you who behaved that way or if it was your partner.

Of course, it's bad enough that you didn't work together as a couple to get both of you out, but it's better to break up than to break the other or yourself.

Do I believe that two children can grow up in a relationship? Yes, but many will not want to stay with the second adult they will see in their marriage. Because it might turn out to be a complete stranger. But there are also cases where two people, having grown up, stay together. It takes good social and financial resources to mitigate the discomfort of this work.

The Skill of Working Independently with One's Sexual Instinct. The Differences Between Male and Female Sexuality

The sexual instinct is a part of our total set of 14 instincts, including territorial, gregarism, death instinct, food instinct, and so on. They govern us in case of danger and are the foundation for structuring all basic forms of life.

The instinct of attraction to the opposite sex has nothing to do with the structure of the feeling of love, it only provides the energy and impulse to get close to someone with whom without the instinct we would be afraid to connect because of our desire for security.

Sexual instinct in women and men works in fundamentally different ways, which makes it difficult for partners to recognise and define instinctive behaviour. Sexuality in men is impulsive and sexuality in women is motivational.

What is the difference?

Impulsive sexuality is expressed in the desire to dominate the object of attraction for no reason, simply because of the attractiveness of the object itself. That is, for the male sexual instinct to kick in, a reaction to the resource virtues in the form of an image, a figure, a scent, a colour is enough. The saturation of the image makes it a resource, and the man evaluates the object's level of desirability depending on which type of resource is more attractive to him.

There is nothing aggressive or narcissistic about this, these are mechanisms inherent in nature, very simple and natural. But they can turn into violence, into evil, if impulsive sexuality is influenced by a woman's childhood libido and she doesn't understand what she is dealing with. The male instinct can also be destructive to the man himself if he, in presenting his impulsive sexuality, expects the woman to have a reciprocal feeling for him.

It will seem to the man that he is giving his all, that he is strong enough to satisfy the woman, and he will not understand why he is not advancing in intimacy with her if he has 'won' her.

It is important for both men and women to understand that love lies far beyond the victories of male impulsive sexuality, and it requires deep emotional skills, psychological competence and knowledge of sexual psychology.

Female motivational sexuality is a natural mechanism that is radically different from that of men. For the female sexual instinct to start working, it takes a lot of reasons—survival conditions, status, perspectives, rituals, life factors of well-being. All of these things really excite women, and it makes no sense to put moralising labels on such female instinctive behaviour.

It is this motivational mechanism of female sexuality that ensures the continuation of the species and the selection of genetics. A sexually healthy woman will never be aroused by a mere sex-for-sex scenario the way a man is, because she will always need arguments. But with those arguments, nothing can stop her libido.

But it must be clear that although a woman's motivational sexuality is strong and deep, it is only a platform for building, with intelligence, emotional development and evolutionary factors, what could be called a higher mental function, that is, love.

Instinct is not yet Love.

The basic instinctive scenarios of man and woman are so very different that on the level of instinct, they cannot create not only love but in principle any real social community. Nature created the sexual instinct solely for the continuation of the species. There is no mechanism in the nature of the material creation of a human in which women and men go much further together than the creation of an offspring.

On the contrary, the less time they stay together, the more active their searching behaviour is, the better chance they have of surviving. But surviving does not mean developing and evolving. Development is necessary only for our souls; flesh does not need it.

The instinctive woman will always need more and more resources and proof of the security of life and space to keep her sexual instinct chained to a man, and to be willing to continue sexual relations with him on a regular basis. And the instinctive man will constantly need proof of his dominance, he will want the woman to give in more and more to him on an ever-increasing list of items. This leads to mutual exhaustion of psyche and physiology.

Gradually, any instinctive relationship begins to degenerate into a form of mutual aggressive attack, as each feel that they are no longer enough of what their partner can provide. Psychologists are right when they say that if you want to change your personal life, it is useless to change your partners, you should change yourself.

But to do this is much more difficult than it may seem. To achieve happiness in a relationship, you need to realign all of your higher neural connections in terms of a more subtle and complex structural organisation.

Exercise

To overcome your sexual instinct, you must take the following steps.

1. For women: write down everything that motivates you to have sexual intercourse with a man.
2. For men: write down everything you want to dominate in and control, to master.
3. for both men and women, to realise what other ways you can use to get it all without using a partner to satisfy your sexual instinct.

Primary sublimation of the sexual instinct. .

The second point from the exercise above is called primary sublimation. Unless your body and psyche are assured that you will give them another way to solve the problem of sex drive in a specific way, there is no way they will allow you to get rid of your animal aggressive attention to the opposite sex.

After the age of 65, it happens that the instinct begins to die out on its own, but then comes the great disappointment of life, because everything we have been chasing all our conscious life, wanting to satisfy ourselves, ceases to have any meaning. One realises that life has not been spent filling the soul, in which an emptiness settles in firmly, and premature psychological aging begins.

Whereas primary sublimation, even done on its own, simply by the power of imagination, already gives a huge relief to the psyche and weakens sexual aggression in favour of higher life priorities, such as creativity, intimacy, education, and so on.

Let's look at an example from a practical private study that will help you understand how these mechanisms work. A 32-year-old lady has an acute phase of frustration on the background of not having a satisfying relationship with a man in every sense. She is not getting good social results and creative achievements because her thoughts are always revolving around the same question—when will she have a partner who will motivate her enough to fulfil her feminine program.

The result is a vicious circle in which she is not socially fulfilled because she cannot find someone she needs, being unable to give such a partner sufficient resources of attraction because she is not socially fulfilled. And those she does attract, do not motivate her to be in a relationship. Her libido sinks into unconscious misery, and she periodically consents to relationships in which only her instincts are fulfilled.

This exacerbates her feeling that she is 'going the wrong way', that love may never happen in her life, and that she will be very disappointed in her feminine destiny.

At the level of instinct, everyone competes with each other, men and women alike. And this competition lowers the work of our psyche even lower, to animal survival. Faced with competition, the lady in our story must either retreat and lose her desirable partner, or display low moral half-animal traits. Both permanently diminish her inner self-worth and self-esteem.

I suggested to this lady that she imagines that she became a wealthy legal heiress in a developed country, by which she immediately gained high social status and recognition of her gender capital there. In other words, I offered her a primary sublimation in the form of an imaginary scenario where she possesses a title and eight million pounds.

My further question is stereotypical—will the task of finding a fiancé and a man right now and immediately remain relevant?

Our client's psyche is in a healthy state, despite her existing emotional distress. Therefore, she immediately answers as any healthy woman would answer, she answers 'no'; she immediately wants different things. She already wants to change her request to the therapist and counsellor. Her libido is at a higher motivational level, and the system of combining herself with a man immediately begins to change.

Against positioning herself as a person with a protected female libido, her self-esteem and her own creative resource grow, since the energy of life and consciousness is no longer so actively absorbed by the centres of sexual survival.

By removing the acuteness of the sexual instinct with primary sublimation, we begin to gently remove the defence mechanisms that have been built up over years of frustration and emotional lack of a man. This is the second important step after primary sublimation.

Exercise

To go through this stage, we need to answer the following questions.

1. How am I experiencing the bitterness of disappointment of not having the right partner in my life for so long?
2. How do I deal with the tension of not feeling satisfied enough?
3. How do I deal with the auto-aggression of feeling lonely?
4. How do I deal with the fear that I might be alone forever and never have a partner?
5. How do I deal with the pressures of a society that, on a collective subconscious level, sees the threat of degeneration in all singles who do not have an offspring or a partner for sex?
6. Am I aware of the confusing situation of my experiences?

The answers to these questions help you become familiar with your own defence strategy, which, like a shell, has grown around the wound of the instinct that eats away at your soul and personality.

Why Temper Your Sexual Instinct?

It's important to understand that our psyche suffers no small amount of torment when consumed by instinct, regardless of whether or not the tension of sexual intercourse is relieved. Unfortunately, the result is the same whether you're locked up at home or you're out clubbing, changing partners.

You will suffer, because, realising the hopelessness of physical copulation, you will constantly feel the lack of something very important, and even the most attractive partner will begin to cause you severe irritation.

If there is no system of development of higher mental functions based on ethics, culture and upbringing in the society and the family, then children who grow up in such communities will become polygamous, will never know the nature of love, and their relationships will always be instinctive.

True love is only possible in a couple where he and she are faithful to each other and have the mental and emotional resources to go through all the stages of love, lasting more than one year.

After the relaxation of protective strategies, one must move on to the phase of awareness of one's individual need for love, first constructing this scenario in the hypothetical abstract conditions of therapy. In other words, one must become acquainted with one's higher needs without the onslaught of the instinct of copulation.

When one becomes aware of the other, more evolved and sublime part of oneself in a relationship, one is no longer interested in the purely searching behaviour of the male or female. It is replaced by the construction of a scenario of life as a whole, and the view of the relationship as part of that scenario, based on shared higher values.

It is not the shortest and fastest way but there is no other ecological way. It is good if the foundations of upbringing have been laid in the family, and the threshold of instinct has been crossed before puberty is complete. But if that did not happen, then you have to understand that you have to start this work yourself at 35, at 45 and at 55.

Outwardly, you can be a cultured person and have a career. But on the level of feelings, you will be torn by conflicts between your desire to be in a couple and the standard that is important to you in a relationship.

If you betray your high standards, you will doom yourself to a lifetime of suffering. If you don't satisfy your desires, you will reach a low level of stability in terms of emotional health and physiological well-being. To combine both desires and standards, it is necessary to combine instincts and developed higher values, and it requires much work in enhancement of consciousness and ability to construct your own life differently.

But, thanks to such work, over time you will stop looking for casual relationships, stop blaming partners, being in despair and feeling depressed. And, gradually, you will begin to notice that now much more interesting people come in your life, with a qualitatively different outlook, and your relationships are initially more tolerant, empathic, deep, open.

The aggression of intense instinct will be replaced by a gentle intimacy and a desire to enrich the world of your loved one with some spiritual values. Control and anxiety will disappear from the relationship, and trust and softness of dialogue will appear. And, believe me, you will shudder to remember your past sexual relationships, in which there was so little warmth, support, care and confidence in the future.

And one day, you will finally see that it is not people who tear themselves apart in their personal lives, but their instincts and the low level of mental development that allows those instincts to dominate. When a developmental relationship is built on the foundation of the sexual instinct, strangely enough, the instinct begins to calm down and seem to fall asleep, trusting you with the goodness of life and the security of the relationship.

It will wake up only in case of illness, attack or severe stress, but that is another story.

Conscious Practice of Tantra—Energy Exchange Healing the Vice of Greed

The Law of Transformation of Energies.

One of the categories of Hindu philosophy, sankhya, describes the three gunas[4] of human's material nature: goodness and heavenly serenity (sattva), violent emotionality and the play of passions (rajas), and finally, the deep abyss of indifference, ignorance and half-animal existence (tamas).

The energy of feelings is subject to the same principle. The primary impulse of tenderness, kindness, understanding, and attraction are pure energies (sattva), bright and carrying only positivity. Later, we begin to experience jealousy, envy, bruised ego, irritation, anger (rajas).

Finally, coldness, strangeness and indifference lead to the lowest manifestations of human nature (tamas). In order not

---

4 The gunas of Sankhya refer to the three basic principles of material nature, the three 'modes of activity' of the illusory energy of maya that condition living beings (jivas). The gunas determine the way of life, the way of thinking and the activities of the soul that they condition.

to fall into negativity and keep our balance, we need to be very delicate and cautious in the actions we take.

Love as the most powerful force on earth pushes all people to do great (moral and not-so-great) things, which generates a great deal of suffering. Just as most wars are initiated by confessional squabbles, so most of our sorrows and heartaches have their origins in love stories.

To ensure that the energy of love does not devolve into one continuous negativity, we need an ethics of sensual balance—a code of conduct that helps create a basis for developing love in a relationship without sacrificing it to negative and hostile mutual attitudes.

Fundamentals of the Ethics of Sensual Balance.

When two people quarrel, there is always someone else who delights in that quarrel. The number one law, therefore, is this: friendship, kinship, and previous relationships represent a lower vibration than a new relationship. Consequently, you cannot introduce friends or former partners into the circle of a couple in love on equal terms with them and give them positions of influence.

Eighty per cent of all divorces and breakups are due to the interference of third parties—relatives, friends, former partners and even children. God created man and woman for each other, and the rest of the world is built around the unity of this binary code, Yin and Yang.

There is an opinion among socionics experts (a scientific field at the crossroads of psychology, sociology and computer science) that true happiness in a couple is only possible between so-called duals when people harmoniously complement each other in personality characteristics (psycho- and socio-types).

Complement, in this case, means that the partners are very different and, at the same time, the specifics of their differences for both is comfortable: for example, one has a strong logic, and the other, a weak one, but it is interesting for them to enhance it and to like it when the partner is logical. In a dual pair, people are often so good together that they really do not need anyone else. Of course, there are friends and family, but usually, such a pair is a closed self-sufficient system.

Another version of the first law—the less action, the less negativity. This is what the concept of honeymoon is for, when the whole world gives way to the couple in their unity, as the quality and purity of the field of love will determine the purity of born thoughts, and thus, the purity of actions and decisions. Unity and awareness in actions generate a minimum amount of negativity that does not obscure the source of love that remains open.

In love, one must listen only to oneself and one's heart, and provide the feeling of love with the freedom of one's decisions. By adopting this principle, we keep our sensual field in its original form. '…It is only in the heart that one can see rightly, what is essential is invisible to the eye'.[5]

The second law of the ethics of sensual balance states that we must verify and guard the purity of love in its intentions and sources. This may not be the beginning of the path of love, but those pseudo-love viruses we discussed earlier.

For example, the virus of sexual instinct, which enters our mental attraction and turns the connection into a state of purely sexual satisfaction. Or the virus of our ego, which

---

5 Antoine de Saint-Exupery. *The Little Prince*.

asserts itself through energy, acceptance and admiration from our partner. Or the virus of the inner teenager's infatuation, who can't stand to be alone, and takes their child's place in the world at all costs, providing themselves with care.

Love of the Two is an Open System That Evolves Forever

A step towards the pure feeling of love.

If all the key obstacles are overcome, and we have two adults who have reached contact with their higher selves and have a vibrant personality, what awaits such a couple in a relationship? A real, most interesting adventure in life awaits them, one that goes through each other's inner world, the difference of potentials, building trust and intimacy and creating a common spiritual world.

Without the energy of love, one will not discover one's divine nature. Coming to love means overcoming all obstacles and vices, achieving an evolutionary level of development and fulfilling God's plan for the higher essence of human.

It must be said that at this level, the understanding of the nature of love is already radically different from what our inner children think of it when they leave the parental home.

So what is the true nature of love?

Love implies our service to it, not its service to us.

Love is the closest state to God within ourselves.

Love encompasses all areas of life, not just the relationship between a man and a woman, between family members or between friends.

Love is ethical and ritualistic.

Approaching the nature of love marks a fundamentally different quality of life in all spheres, not just interpersonal relationships. The notion that love resides only in the realm of relationships is a child's perception of the feeling of love, its projection onto other people, because, as we remember, a child's life depends entirely on relationships.

Love lives in the relationship zone of human's consciousness with their spirit, their immortal self, and from there, it builds a space of realisation outwards. If one's expectation of love is associated with being rewarded in the world of men and being spared from misfortune, then one will meet within oneself their child and all the perversions of modern civilisation that accompany the culture of infantile consumerism.

Knowing true love discumbers of consumerist attitudes and gives one an attitude of co-creation with reality.

Accepting Love

It is important for a woman to create and develop her field of love as she understands it. For a man, it is important to find the field of love in a woman, to guard this field and to be assured of the right to be in this field. This is the fundamental difference between men's and women's image of love at the stage when their relationship has already approached the phase of love and has unfolded in it.

If a boy has not had a trusting relationship with his mother, he may push a woman out of her creating field of love, trying to create on his own the standard of what love and relationships should be, in his opinion. As a result of this strategy, he can never, in the slightest degree, experience satisfaction or peace. On the contrary, his degree of tension will increase, and so will the number of shifting relationships.

Similarly, a woman who seeks love from outside herself incorporates the male strategy associated with her sense of insecurity coming from her father.

For a woman, resourcefulness is at the forefront of her value system, and for a man, potency. If a woman lacked warmth and intimacy with her mother, she may expect resources of love from a man, but not be the source of them herself.

To summarise the difficulties of love, if we look for love in the fulfilment of social, familial, generic, and personal tasks, we will end up with the inevitable disappointment of the relationship itself and of our role in it. The discipline of love begins with a total recognition of its value in and of itself, regardless of the nuances that our whole human nature of related needs gives it.

The painful subtlety of love is precisely that in its pure form, by itself as a need, it does not exist in the human world. It is a product of ready-made mature spiritual structures that are above human basic daily needs.

If you are not ready for love, there is nothing wrong with it. You can experience it bypassing the world of human needs—in art, music, nature, all manifestations of the Creator. This is far better than mixing glimpses of this feeling with others that must be realised in very different ways than love asserting itself.

The Genius of Love.

How does the genius of love manifest itself?

Why does love itself have such tremendous value?

Love, when confronted with conditions, can never withstand them. But it will be able to transcend those conditions and outgrow them. Love is the greatest gift of earthly life, and it does not exist in the spiritual world as it is given to us here.

We experience love on earth very acutely precisely because it is here as a message from heaven, as a contrast to our earthly nature, and there is nothing stronger than this contrast between our flesh and the spiritual experience of love. The fusion of carnal attraction and love gives us the ability to transcend all our limited earthly nature.

It is impossible to aspire to love out of earthly urges, but it is possible to grow to love out of them.

Love spiritualises the most perfect forms available—the highest archetypes, unselfish desires, the purity of sacrifice and service, beautiful dreams.

Levels of Need for Love

The level of need for love is determined by the evolutionary level of our consciousness. For one, the need for love is a return to a secure parental relationship. For another, it is the complete dissolution of one's ego into the flows of the Creator's love. Between these two poles lie the destinies of people as diverse as each person's unique place in the unified space of love.

In the course of life, in relation to the feeling of love, we go through the following stages:

1) merging with love, when it is the source of all our life and all its benefits (consciousness does not separate itself from love);

2) differentiation of our self from the feeling of love and comprehension of its various forms (this stage affects mind and ego in us, and therefore, passes rather painfully because in the process of cognition mind literally dissects feelings, separating them from our self, and we may practically lose contact with them);

3) sharing feelings with others on the basis of differentiated perception (harmony of mind and feelings arises);

4) creating the feeling of love as a holistic state and transmitting it to others (full awareness and regulation of the flow of feelings in unity with the mind emerges);

5) return to the merging, when love again becomes the whole world for us.

We experience similar stages both within the relationship development cycles of the couple and within our own life and age cycles. The second stage (differentiation of the self from the feeling of love) often coincides with the period of social separation and with the second or third year of the life cycle of the adult couple. Sometimes differentiation of the self in love may lead to cleavage with love or to displacement of all forms of experience of love.

In such a situation, supportive therapy will be needed to help strengthen our connection to the central meaning of all life. Therapy will help us to understand that the feeling of suffering from seeming separation from love is only a necessary experience and a temporary phase in which we learn how different forms of love can be available to an evolved person.

It is not advisable to 'move too far' away from love, or else, as the energy of isolation accumulates, the force of attraction to the desired state of love may push us into a merger at the level of the destruction of all degrees of freedom.

The journey through the cycles of love should be seen as an evolutionary practice of development, not as a constant return to the starting point of fusion. Our mastery of spiritual evolution in love is balanced by the ability to be in contact with love in all its hypostases.

At the highest level is an entity capable, like an Arhat[6], of bringing new colours, vibrations, and signs of being into the unified field of love as a whole. By touching, to give back this love—with our gaze, with our consciousness, with our presence. As the great Rumi taught, carry the culture of the heart as the altar of Love and put nothing above it.[7]

One can increase one's level of development by realising for oneself the nature of one's need for love.

I want love. Why?

Or, if I am love, why?

Or, if I love someone, what does that mean?

---

6 Arhat (Sanskrit for 'worthy'): In Buddhism, a person who has attained complete liberation from the perception of the world by egocentric consciousness, which prevents them, from experiencing the world as it really is, and who has emerged from the 'wheel of rebirths'. A person who, while still alive, has reached incomplete Nirvana, that is, the perfect, supreme state of the soul, characterised by absolute tranquillity, absence of any passions and egoistic movements.

7 One day a man came to the house of his Beloved. He knocked on the door.

"Who is there?" The Beloved asked.

The man replied, "It is I who love you."

"Go away," said the Beloved. "You are not really in love."

Years later, the man came to his Beloved's door again and knocked.

"Who is there?" The Beloved asked.

This time the man answered, "It is you."

"Now that you are me," replied the Beloved. "You may enter."

Muhammad Rumi was a prominent Persian Sufi poet.

If I want love, I feel it in myself and carry it to others simply because love is the only form of divine existence.

And a very different kind of love happens when someone wants to survive and relies on the field of love to be accepted and not become rejected. Perhaps such love would be a sign of passing through the differential stage of a relationship with it.

The negative motivation to love is just as strong as the positive one. On one edge are those who desire love, and on the other are those who put it above themselves as an archetype, as a power, as the face of the Creator, seeing in it all a chance to manifest their service of love through the wisdom of actions and the beauty of words.

At the highest level, we live in the trinity and perfection of love, wisdom and beauty. And it is love that is the driving force that gives wisdom its vitality and beauty its power and perfection.

As we open the book of destinies, we see that the path of love is equal to the path of the heart, the path of destiny and all meanings.

At the very beginning of its evolution, the Soul learns to love by receiving. It learns to take love, to be drunk with it like a nectar, to be dependent and seeking. This is the first phase of merging. It is needed to learn love from those who give it to us, through service to them.

The seeker of love is conditioned by the vast array of things, events, and signs that symbolise this feeling and serve to explain belonging and attraction.

Developed, old souls, love very differently; they are no longer conditioned by anything and do not take love, but give it away. And even if they do take it, they do it in such a way that you become incredibly happy. At the highest level of development, we are capable of simultaneously transmitting, perceiving and differentiating the feeling of love.

That is, to synthesise and experience the totality of this powerful state of receptivity. This is the phase of unconditioned contact with love, when all of our capacities are actualised simultaneously.

The delightful experience of unconditioned love gives us ecstatic encounters and relationships in all aspects of the Creator. There is no longer a need to hold or seek love; it becomes the air, the space and the reality of which our whole life consists.

Between those who take love and those who give it away, there are often mutual alliances. They bear little resemblance to happiness in its pure form, and are rather discipleship and the advancement of the plan of evolution towards its realisation.

In the middle are people who equally seek love and give it away. This is the most difficult path, but it is still much more beautiful than the path to love in the state of working through generic energies or projections.

People who give and receive love in equal measure may often change partners, playing the role of either the giver or the receiver.

This will be going on until the Soul moves into the state of giving, and then the partners in the cosmic dance of love will be those who will serve in the acceptance of love, giving their life and destiny undividedly for the benefit of accepting the bearer of love.

At the next stage of evolution, those who give love again begin to accept it from those who stand on a higher step, while those who previously accepted it learn to give it to those who are weaker than them.

We are constantly changing roles and tasks, and this is the experience of comprehending the different qualities of love for the sake of the one ultimate goal of attaining love as a self-sufficient form of the free manifestation of God in us.

Until we reach this level, we go through all the stages of comprehending love again and again, experiencing births and deaths, meetings and partings, changing objects of love and ways of interacting with them.

Exercise

Each person, looking at the list of phases of love, is able to write someone's name in front of each of the five points. It can be the name of the person with whom you have experienced a particular phase of love as deeply as possible, the name of a teacher or a role model, the name of a character from a reference encounter that took place in a particular energy field.

1) Describe the main feelings that you experienced with this person. For example, at the first stage of merging, it may be the grandmother who raised you, or the man with whom you had your first experience of love. Or the first time you went out in public, if you are a musician and experience merging with music as love. You will have one or more feelings opposite each phase.

2) Write for each phase, what facets of love did you discover through this experience? What was love like for you at each of these stages?

3) Compose an essay, combining all your stories and experiences with the theme 'My Path of Love'. Highlight and describe the main changes that happened to you in the love story of destiny: how life changed, how you yourself changed, and what happened to your feelings and life scripts.

4) Reread your essay. See if at least one paragraph has your name and relationship story with self-love in it? If not, try to figure out what happens to your destiny the moment you refuse to love yourself, when you are willing to go through life with love hand in hand while crossing out love for yourself. What does that tell you? And does this kind of love happen, or have you split yourself off from the holistic feeling of love in which you also exist for yourself. If you notice such splitting, what causes it?

5) Write an essay about what qualities and achievements of yours cause people to love you, and what you love about yourself.

6) Describe your future love story in all five phases, imagining yourself at the age of around 60, the age of spiritual maturity, showing the result of your whole life journey. What life capital of love would you like to accumulate in your destiny?

Creating a Love Secret.

Collect your materials. It is even better to put them in a beautiful box. Take a look at what and how you wrote your works. If they were not beautifully designed, transfer the content to an aesthetically pleasing notebook. Buy and place in the box items or jewellery that symbolise tenderness and caring for you, a pleasant sense of loving empathy and opening your heart.

You can meditate and heal your heart with these items as you continue the practice of writing down your love story. Such an inheritance, passed on to your descendants, will be a true treasure for your family. But perhaps at the end of the journey, you will realise that all paths of love lead to the Creator, and you will leave only one record, which will go something like this:

"Lord, thank You for Your love."

Building a Couple's Relationship with Kin and Society

Duty of Kin to Love.

A sense of ancestral belonging gives a person a sense of exceptional acceptance and intimacy, even if it doesn't feel that way on the level of a personal relationship. Even when there is much discord, indifference and resentment in the family, when there are isolated loved ones, nevertheless, every kinsman is absolutely important, irreplaceable, and part of the blood and life of all other family members.

The kinship structure demands complete and undivided belonging, loyalty, service, presence. And these obligations do not arise for nothing, they are given in exchange for the most important thing—the right to be born, the right to life.

Our kins have the most complicated relationship with both the feeling of love and the ability to express it. Rather, habitual blood scripts teach us to fight and compete for love, to extract and protect it in every possible way, to turn it into private property and to do other things that make the feeling of love more and more elusive, gradually melting into the mists of complex experiences and low energies.

So in today's world, we can no longer talk about love within kin, we talk about the duty of kin to love. People think they are owed love. In fact, their kin duty to love have already grown so large that even if all family members put all their good feelings into one basket, it will be difficult for them to pay off, so to speak, all the unloving accumulated by the generations of the family in relation to each other and to the world as a whole.

This fact makes the family structures consumeristic, hungry for intimacy and material goods, all the energy that nourishes, heals and fills. Entering any kin space in today's world becomes an equation with many unknowns.

No one knows at what moment and to whom love will be lacking, and what kind of military action a person will take in order to get hold of the nourishing power of kin support and make everyone give out at least one drop of love for ten litres of blood.

It is for this reason that many people in today's world live alone. They are simply unable to be donors of love in a shortage that literally has no end, so deep and profound is the hunger of community members or blood relatives for acceptance, understanding, provision, care and nurturing. Once fate and the feeling of love bring a man and a woman together and they become a couple, the laws of kinship and family begin to apply to them.

It is not easy to find a balance between the love of the couple and the requirement of the tribal system to fulfil duty. Usually, love is sacrificed, and the two begin to work off debts within the family. The task of love is left out of the equation and usually, donor structures are sought on the side to 'solve' it.

Lovers or mistresses sacrifice their part of love, the interests of their own kind, when stronger partners, bound by strong ties to their families, subordinate them to themselves, making them objects of sexual intimacy. Such donation of the feeling of love always ends badly; and it never began well.

It is possible to get out of the war of kin with love and for love only through conscious action, by understanding the tasks of one's kin and writing them out on a separate sheet— next to the tasks of love, the tasks of one's spirit and one's tasks as a person in the existing social reality. There is a very important step in this work.

Remember that there is no limit to the kin's hunger for love, and we need to balance all evolutionary goals to find balance in how much of ourselves and our energy we are willing to give to our intimate relationships with our kin and family members.

Exercise

Answering to the following questions will help you work through the relationship of love in the kin.

1. Have I received everything I need as a child in my kin?
2. If I am feeling deficient, how can I make up for it from being an adult?
3. What kind of love energy has always been lacking in our family? Understanding, patience, support, nourishment, gifts, participation, hugs?
4. Can I stop being a child in my kin and take the place of an adult who will be a father and a mother on a soul level for family members?

5. How strong are my grievances against my family and kin as a whole? How strong is my disrespect for family members?
6. Is it true that my family members wished me to be alone, or do I myself voluntarily choose isolation?
7. Wouldn't it make more sense to learn to keep my distance in difficult situations in order to maintain balance and a desire for cooperation?
8. How can I end the war of love in my family and in my kin?

Love as the Basic Energy of Development.

The energy of love is the basic life force without which no structure can develop. The energy of love gives the basis for the creation of everything, and if it is not there, nothing will happen. You can make up all the business plans and strategies you want, but they can all come to life only by the power of nourishing love, in which the relationships of everyone around you play a role, and above all those whom we consider close by blood or simply include in our sensual circle of communication.

Creating our own sensual circle and distributing within it the resources of influence, power, and balance with a healthy attitude of a warm heart towards each person is a task for a well-developed emotional intelligence. No one can live without such a sensual circle of life, on which our emotional health is directly dependent.

The Spiritual Choice of Building a Couple Object. Allocating a Special Spiritual Resource to Couple Building

The spiritually mature person as the subject of love is irreplaceable, unique, unrepeatable for true love. True love can be seen as a kind of guarantee of infinite affection. It is true that King Solomon claimed that everything in the world passes. While respectfully agreeing with the great thinker, let us make just one clarification within our context.

Yes, various states, experiences, and emotions do pass, just as passion, obsession, and sexual excitement pass. The quenched libido fades, falling in love is altogether fleeting.

But a spiritual revelation, in which one turns to the spiritual personality of the other, is experienced by oneself as well. And it is experienced infinitely from the moment of the emergence of this spiritual revelation. True love as a couple's experience of a common spiritual being is timeless, unlike bodily and mental sexuality.

The love of spiritually mature people is more than a state of feeling. The spiritual essence of the beloved is unique, it is beyond time and space, and therefore infinite and incomprehensible. The 'idea' of a person, what a lover sees in them, belongs to immortality. The true lover is so filled with the essence of the other person that his or her own reality becomes secondary.

The physicality of the beloved is so unimportant to love that it survives their physical death and continues until the death of the one who loves. This is why love is stronger than death.

Love is directed specifically towards the spiritual person of the beloved, towards the fullness of their uniqueness (for these are the manifestations of the spiritual person). But in order to see the other, one must first see oneself and realise one's uniqueness.

Love is characterised by a mature idealisation. It is associated with the exceptional place of a partner in one's own soul compared to anyone else. With a reverent attitude towards them, with a desire to admire them, to rejoice in their words, in their gestures, simply in their presence.

Imagine the author of the book sitting for hours in the mosque where stands the sarcophagus of Sultan Hürrem, laid to rest by her lover for many centuries, and tranquilised at the entrance to eternity in the arms of love.

Imagine the luxurious chambers of a Sufi harem, where the author lived as the Sheikh's bride for two years of her life, and received initiations of the most exquisite Sufi traditions of joining the souls of a man and a woman in worship of the Creator.

Imagine that you, too, as the author of this book, had the unique opportunity to hear the voice of a wise Sheikh recounting the amazing spiritual Sufi traditions and rituals. Today this wonderful man has left his mortal shell and reunited with the Creator in the chambers of Divine Love. But his voice seems to resound to this day, and will resound for hundreds of years, warming and guiding the hearts of the living.

The Words of Sufi Jalal ad-Din Loras.

I think we all have that experience when we see someone for the first time, but we feel like we've known them for a very long time. My father and teacher explained this phenomenon to me when I was about 10 years old. "Before we came to earth, we were in heaven. The person you met in heaven was very close to you. Now that your soul has entered their body and their soul has entered the body, you cannot know the body, but you can know the soul."

Maybe we were born to our mother and father before we came to Earth. Maybe we met each other many times, shared something, opened our hearts to each other. Here and with Astara, we recognised each other through our eyes.

What are eyes? They are like grains. When you look at a little grain, you can see all the corn, all the seeds. God's eyes can see it before it happens. And every one of us has that ability.

Our wealth is the love of God. Our happiness consists in serving people, God's creatures. If you continue to seek the truth in yourself and anywhere else, try to be happy. Because God is with you. If you carry this faith in you everywhere and always, your vision of the world and your love will become different, you will find great patience.

I am still not there, and so I always break down. But I don't give up; I don't want to give up because I have the desire. I know that I will be God's friend. Every day, I find myself in hundreds of different situations, for I can't see what's right in front of me. And the first thing I must always remember: there is God, and I ask for His hand for support.

And I go on, and I fall again. It's not easy. But we need to go, we need to love, we need to go through challenges and sacrifices in order to achieve gold within ourselves. We need to let the challenges be.

God brings us to the right place at the right time, and we become happier.

God is with us now and always. With our love, harmony and beauty.

Fifty years ago, my father decided to spread this teaching to all Western civilisation, not dividing its representatives into men and women, because we are all part of God's creation and there are no differences between us. The light of God is the same in all of us. It is true that it takes forty years for a man to discover his own essence. For women, one night is enough.

In Western society, women are more devoted to God than men. We men are probably more distrustful of life. We have egos or attitudes of mind that we hide. Maybe we are afraid of 'losing our dignity'. But to prevent this from happening, we must remember what every religion says: don't lie. And we must learn, first of all, not to lie to ourselves. Then perhaps we can come to God more quickly, like women.

Rumi said: "Be happy as you are. Be honest with yourself. By lying you destroy your purity, your light, which is always needed, in this world and in the other. God doesn't care how much time we spend worshipping, He doesn't need it. But He asks: *Bring me a pure heart filled with light.*"

God loves us more than we can imagine. If someone is hurt, God immediately feels that pain as if it were his own. This is not a fairy tale or an exaggeration. He never wants to hurt us.

This is the God I pray to. What does it mean to pray? To love and be grateful, create harmony all around. To approach the divine light that lives in the heart step by step. Each of us is the pure heart of God. We seek the truth in ourselves. God is reaching out to all of us to help and bring us to Himself. Why? Because we deserve it. If we didn't, we wouldn't be here.

All religions teach us that God is 'up there' somewhere. What God is really saying is, "I am a treasure, I want to be known. And that is the reason I created everything that exists in the universe. But I Myself cannot fit in the universe I created because it is too small for Me. However, I can fit in the heart of the beloved like you."

The real God does not live in India, Jerusalem, Mecca, or anywhere else on earth. God's true home is in our heart.

From time to time, turn your eyes to your pure heart and welcome God there. This does not require any great knowledge or experience. Just say, "Hello, God, I love You. Please give me your hand, bring me to You." And you will receive peace, harmony and beauty from the Creator.

Love and ecstasy is our way. All of us have had excitement, rapture, boiling like volcanic lava from love. It is ecstasy. It is beautiful to love someone, and to always want to be with the one you love.

Sufi Jálal ad-Din Rumi said, confessing his love for a woman.

I want to tell you a word without a tongue,
It's not for your ears to judge.
It is for your ears only, not those of strangers,
Though it be spoken in the presence of many.
Come, my beauty, above words and measure!
Break up the darkness of prayer and longing without a trace.

With you, prayer is all that serves as a sign of faith.

Without you, prayer itself is but a sign.

Do not believe that I no longer long for thee.

And I am not saddened by your absence:

Thy love's guilt I have absorbed a part of,

That I have had and will have thy love for ever.[8]

Sufi Jalal ad-Din Loras, his descendant, says, confessing his love for Astara.

"…We have turned another leaf on the calendar of life, and another year has flown by, as if carried away by the wind of time.

Time moves differently for everyone. It crawls like a turtle for those who wait. It swiftly flies like a seagull for those who are afraid. It turns into an endless road for those who mourn and a short bridge for those who rejoice. It turns into eternity for those who love.

It has been a wonderful year. At times, we have lost a part of ourselves with the passing of our loved ones.

At times, we became even more whole with the arrival of someone in our lives.

At times, we cried and suffered for nothing, and at other times, we cried because we were hurting someone.

But when we laughed, our laughter was heard by the whole world, in which the sun rose.

And it also happened that we couldn't forgive someone or give up something.

We will value our time and spend it carefully, giving the lion's share of it to our loved ones and those we love.

---

8 Translated by F. Korsch.

I ask you, with the support of the Most High, to enter my heart. And I, your beloved, will be happy forever. I want you to know and be convinced every second that I love you. I want you to never be sad, and I want you to teach me the same. I give you my heart and soul so that you can find the happiness you deserve. This is the strongest of all my desires.

My heart is now separated from yours, and it is an unbearable pain that overwhelms me completely, making me weak as a blade of grass in the wind. Come to me to make me healthy and strong. Let me wait for you. Make up your mind and, come.

My love, I love you so much and miss you so much.

May all my beautiful days always be yours, always bright and spiritually uplifting.

We will have many joyful smiles. I believe in you, I hope in you and I will always love you.

You are my happiness, my tenderness! I think of you every second.

My darling, my treasure, my life, my Astara…"

'...Hayat takviminde bir yaprak daha devirdik ve bir yıl daha zamanın rüzgarıyla savrulup uçup gitti.

Zaman herkes için farklı ilerliyor. Bekleyenler için kaplumbağa gibi sürünür. Korku duyanlar için hızlı kanatlı bir martı gibi süpürürür. Yas tutanlar için uçsuz bucaksız bir yola, sevinenler için kısa bir köprüye dönüşür. Sevenler için sonsuzluğa dönüşür.

Harika bir yıl oldu. Bazen sevdiklerimizin gidişiyle bir parçamızı kaybederiz.

Bazen birilerinin hayatımıza girmesiyle daha da bütünleşiriz.

Bazen boşuna ağladık ve acı çektik, bazen de birini incittiğimiz için.

Ama güldüğümüzde, kahkahamız Güneş'in doğduğu tüm dünya tarafından duyuldu.

Ayrıca birini affedemedemediğimiz ve bir şeyi reddedemedemediğimiz de oldu.

Zamanımıza değer vereceğiz ve özenle harcayacağız, aslan payını sevdiklerimize ve sevdiklerimize vereceğiz.

Yüce Allah'ın desteğiyle kalbime girmeni istiyorum. Ve ben, sevgilin, sonsuza kadar mutlu olacağım. Seni sevdiğimi her saniye bilmeni ve buna ikna olmanı istiyorum. Asla üzülmemeni istiyorum ve sen de bana aynısını öğrettin. Sana hak ettiğin mutluluğu vermek için kalbimi ve ruhumu veriyorum. Bu, tüm arzularımın en güçlüsü.

Kalbim şimdi seninkinden ayrı ve bu dayanılmaz bir acı, beni tamamen kaplıyor ve rüzgarda bir ot sapı gibi beni güçsüzleştiriyor. Beni sağlıklı ve güçlü kılmak için bana gel. Seni beklememe izin ver. Kararını ver ve gel.

Aşkım seni çok seviyorum ve çok özlüyorum.

Bütün güzel günlerim hep senin olsun, hep aydınlık ve ruhsal olarak yüksek olsun.

Birçok neşeli gülümsememiz olacak. Sana inanıyorum, sana umut ediyorum ve seni her zaman seveceğim.

Sen benim mutluluğumsun, hassasiyetim! Her saniye seni düşünüyorum.

Canım, hazinem, hayatım, Astaram...'

Spiritualised Eros

Spiritual love can be described in the language of symbols.

Imagine a temple in which the rays of the sun are breaking through the domed vaults and falling on the train of the bridal gown. This is the time when the Lord enters as the third party into the relationship.

Imagine the journey of the pilgrim who returns from Mount Athos to his beloved and brings her from the holy mountain a golden cross studded with diamonds, emeralds and kisses. His grown-up hair and beard flutter in the wind. His ship docks at the island of Thessaloniki, where she awaits him, pregnant with his fourth child.

Imagine the journey of a shaman who, at night, leads his beloved by the hand through the mountains of the Altai. He shows her the eyes of an owl glowing in the darkness. He gathers magic herbs, which give their power to the sound of a tambourine, becoming for the beloved a bed of demigods, drowned in the glow of the stars, the moon, and the first rays of the sun rising over the mountain peaks.

All this is spiritualised Eros, creating an act of love not just between two people, but in the space between the Earth and the Cosmos, transmitting the power of his energy through the female spiritualised Anima. The radiant Anima is so relaxed, malleable and gentle that her earthly balance can hold any volume of cosmic energy of her great Animus. She is to him an earthly chalice and conduit of divine energy to will and power on the earthly level.

The revelation of the spiritualised Eros and the divine Anima leads to the awakening in partners of inner magicians, omnipotent, recognising the primacy of the Creator, and perceiving the universe as their home.

In this scenario, people have gone through all the previous stages of passion and the triumph of personality in a relationship, and experience a cosmic encounter with each other's spirit as a guide in making love with the Creator himself. The ecstasy and freedom experienced in such a couple pass with them into other worlds after the death of the physical body.

From this point in the relationship, the couple goes through the higher path of White Tantra, where every step, action and aspect is deeply ritualised.

Spiritual Rituals of Love. The seven keys are:

1. Renouncing personal use of each other in a relationship.
2. The clearing of one's mind.
3. Inviting the creator as a third party into the relationship.
4. The ritual of uniting the two into one in spirit.
5. Ritual of inviting spiritual energies into the unity of two.
6. Common We as a conductor of divine energies.
7. Transition to the divine state of consciousness. Receiving the keys to nirvana.

The author of the book went through more than 30 rituals—kora—sign circumambulation of the first floor of temples in Tibet and Nepal. In the process of performing these rituals, the seeker of spiritual enlightenment, blessed by the abbot to the sounds of mantras, views their consciousness and samsara with their inner gaze. The movement signifies the clearing of one's consciousness from samsara and the exit into nirvana.

Going through the kora, the seeker ascends through three floors to the very top of the temple. Each floor symbolises one of the worlds, and usually, there are three, as in all religious teachings: the material, the social and the world of the Creator. On the uppermost floor is an image of the wheel of samsara, which is contrastingly filled with the energies of Yin and Yang, and symbolises the final union of the male and female in the Creator for enlightenment.

The final tantra is the complete attainment of balance in harmony between light and shadow. Shadow symbolises the feminine, light the masculine.

Tibetan temples very symbolically reflect all principles of the structure of the universe. And through comprehension of this symbolism, we get to the fact that liberation from samsara is possible only through love. And it is achieved in the expanded consciousness by keeping the balance of all things in the masculine and feminine.

By refusing to comprehend the stages of maturation of the psyche through the natural stages of being, a person can ruin many of their lives by breaking their perception of love as the highest form of spiritual practice and falling to the level of animal instincts. But it is only through the realisation of love as such in all its forms that one can rise to the top, going through life after life of similar stages, cycles, and initiations.

The author of the book, contemplating the ancient thangkas in the segments of the ceiling painting, symbolising all aspects of the mergence of the male and the female, was in an incredible spiritual ecstasy, as were hundreds of thousands of monks before her and millions after her. Often the top floor of a temple has only a roof and no walls, and the temple is in a huge valley surrounded by mountains 3,000 metres above sea level.

These heights, majesty, purity, mergence and synthesis bring one's consciousness in life to full enlightenment of heart and consciousness.

As one descends from the upper floor, one returns again to the earthly atmosphere of the temple, where monks in red robes sit and chant mantras. During the meal, the consciousness, as far as possible, returns to ordinary life, but in the heart forever remains the light and nectar of bliss of perfect love, which cannot be held back by anything and which becomes one with the person and with the soul.

When the author lived in the harem of Sheikh Jalal al-Din Loras in Konya, he would come every morning and bring a rose from the garden. When the Sheikh was gone, both these roses and the rituals remained as a symbol of the possibility of a form of love in which the spirit and the way of human become one. The rose in the symbolism of Sufi culture represents the perfection of the sacrificial consciousness of the lover, who forgets himself when he sees his beloved.

Wherever in the world we go in search of sacred mysteries, we will find ourselves in an atmosphere of the perfect love as the pinnacle of spiritual and psychic practice.

Eventually, you come to understand and accept this truth or go back to samsara (to its lowest layers) until you learn the art of perfecting your heart in Divine love step by step.

The Words of Sufi Jalal ad-Din Loras.

Any mystic, without separating himself in any way from the laws of his religion, treats people more warmly than a religious dogmatist. Mysticism concentrates more on love than on religious institutions. Mystics develop special techniques for clearing the heart from darkness. I want to share such practices with you.

One way or another, sooner or later, the selfishness and cruelty of the world around us brings darkness to the human heart. But mystics have found a way to clear the heart of darkness. We ask the Creator of the Universe, 'Please forgive us for the past, present, and future mistakes we make. Help us to correct those mistakes in reality. Please forgive us, for You are divinely generous'.

The whole essence of this appeal to the Creator is encapsulated in the Arabic word 'estagfurullah', Embrace your heart, straighten your back, and repeat 'estagfurullah'. Clear your heart, your chest. Send this appeal to Mother Earth. After that, lift the energy upwards, to the divine level, bring the divine light into your heart with the words 'estagfurullah'.

By doing this practice, you purify yourself and your loved ones, raising their souls along with yours to the divine level. You receive God's light and share it with your loved ones. You share your generosity. The concepts of 'I' and 'they' disappear. There is only WE—one heart, one body, one mind.

Placing our hands on our knees and repeating 'estagfurullah', swaying slightly, from left to right and right to left, we ask forgiveness of all the people of Earth.

Islamic mysticism was born twelve hundred years ago, and the experience accumulated over the centuries is embodied in special body movements which, for example, make blood flow downward and then rise to the brain and is distributed throughout the body. All such practices are performed to music in the form of a dance.

Each of the 12 schools of Sufism has its own form. Each school worships a particular personality. A person has 12 different levels of character. Not all depts of different schools wear skirts and whirl. Not every school has people who sit and then start jumping and screaming. Some schools do what they do by listening to their heart.

Some think very loudly while doing dhikr—remembering God through calling the divine name. The one who wishes to embrace the way of mevlevi has a heart that responds to this teaching.

If a young man comes to us, we ask, 'Do your parents know about what you have chosen?'.

If it is an adult, we ask, 'Do you have patience?'.

After giving an affirmative answer to these questions, the person is placed in the room that serves as the kitchen for the school. We say, 'A new gift to God has arrived at the school', and we cover the newcomer with a deer skin. The deer is always thirsty. The gland of this animal produces musk with a particularly pleasant aroma.

The newcomer fasts for three days. He does nothing, just observes what happens in the kitchen. The kitchen in the mevlevi is the point where the teaching begins, because it symbolises the place where one wants to prepare food or be prepared for others. After three days, the kitchen bashi asks the novices if they want to continue. If the answer is again affirmative, the novices spend the next 18 days working in the kitchen: serving, washing, and cleaning.

After a total of 21 days, they are asked the same question, and if they want to continue, they get new clothes. The challenge begins, lasting 1001 days. There are 18 jobs to be done during these 1001 days in order to prepare the soul, develop patience, and form an understanding of the path. During this time, the teachers of the school are watching them very closely to see what kind of gift they are bringing from heaven to earth.

The man has no idea that he will be a great musician, but the teacher sees it in his eyes. The boy from the village who has never picked up a pen can become the best calligrapher in the world. Or, for example, he has never seen woodcarving, but he could be a skilled carver. Or he could be a scholar of any discipline, religion, history.

Hence the name, school. You are educated and trained, discovering what you are be capable of. What gift God has sent with you to Earth.

The last of the jobs is comparable to cleaning a neglected latrine. It is to smash the ego, its desires, in order to make a man humble. But these days, you have gold bracelets on your hands. After all, you are a scholar, a musician, a carver, a calligrapher, you name it. If you have the ability, you can become a whirling dervish or a dervish musician. You will be initiated in whatever you are good at.

If you will be a musician, you will play for the whirling dervishes. You will pray to God by chanting His name in silence with your right hand up and your left hand down, which means: "God, give me light, I will be a bridge for You to bring it to the people on Earth."

If you suddenly break down on any of these 1001 days (even the last day), but want to continue, you need to start over. You are given a small room, and your life becomes celibate, that is, the life of a servant of God. Or you can leave the school, get married, go into business, do anything you want, but still practice. You are part of the school, you just don't live in it.

Mevlevi order is part of Islam, one of the 12 Sufi schools, different from the rest. We turn in all directions in the name of God. Each of us has the ability through the name of the Creator to connect with him.

The Destructive Effects of an Immature Ego on Love.

Anyone's ego is capable of destroying even the most beautiful, promising, and prospective love relationship. It is the immature, unstable, unrealised ego that brings its pent-up ambition into a relationship. Someone articulated the secret of his long successful marriage this way: "When we got married, we were unequal both socially and financially; but I told myself that since we were becoming a couple, at that point we should recognise our equality."

That is, if two people have entered into a relationship and come to live together, they must accept a position of equality and decide all matters on the basis that neither of them has an advantage over the other. Otherwise, when one emphasises one's advantages, accumulates those advantages and does not share them, creating an imbalance, it becomes a vivid manifestation of a sick ego that does not want love, but is trying to fulfil a self-assertion scenario.

When a loving person begins to feel that the person next to them, and at their expense, is being self-asserted, playing out scenarios of ego defence, their positions, their status, the truly loving heart is obliged to close down and move away, because the rules of love stop working in such territory.

An encounter with a cold ego instead of a loving heart always leaves a deeply traumatic impression, creates a mass of control and mistrust, generates fears, and interferes with the exchange of energies. You have to learn to recognise in time that you are being offered an ego instead of a heart and soul that are ready to work.

The consumerist attitude of the unprocessed ego to love is a violation of divine laws and principles. Love owes nothing to anyone. It is we who owe it, as a higher form of being and consciousness than the one in which all mankind lives today. We must learn from love to develop our heart—this is its purpose at the most basic level.

Without love, our heart remains undeveloped; it does not work, we fall behind in evolution and lose the right to be human, a being who stands at the foot of divine consciousness and strives to move into a world higher than that of instinct and the constant struggle for existence.

People who are inflamed by the fiery element of their egos find it very difficult to calm down. And more often than not, they cannot calm down at all until they have lived half a century and it is clear that their war has come to an end. They will be cold, aloof individuals, distanced in relationships, tormented deep down by false sentimental experiences that have nothing to do with love.

Surprisingly, it is people with huge, overinflated egos and shrivelled, undeveloped hearts who suffer more than anyone else from their own romanticisation, sentimentality, and exaggerated attention to feelings and emotions that are not in balance with a wise soul.

This sentimentality replaces their deep work of love, their attention to the soul, their desire for the triune human essence—body, soul and spirit—to be fulfilled in relationships and to begin to rule consciousness through the heart.

Some scholars believe that the objective gender difference is that men are entitled to be less sensitive, while women have a greater emotional responsibility for relationships and for maintaining sensual intimacy. But what if we look more closely at a man as a creature of God? Aren't his erogenous zones just as sensitive as a woman's? And some men are even more sensitive and sensual than women!

All our differences from each other in this matter are not due to gender but to individual differences. We are all different, and sensitivity can be incomprehensibly different from person to person, regardless of their gender.

Signs of an unstable ego in a love relationship:

- being categorical and unable to make concessions;
- pressure and desire to solve all issues unilaterally;
- deprivation of the partner's sense of being loved, refusal to accept and affirm the partner's importance;
- prolonging conflict situations;
- postponing important decisions and refusing to discuss the couple's actual needs;
- inability to overcome their emotional closeness in the relationship;
- inattention to the subtle psychological features of the partner's individuality.

The tougher a person's position in a relationship is, the more unstable, repressed and clamped his or her ego-structure is. Because of its internal instability, the ego seeks to dominate in order to gain power and influence from external sources instead of internal. But feeding from external sources always brings only temporary relief, further increasing the dependence on the false influence of others.

With each act of demanding and asserting, the feeling of dissatisfaction and estrangement from the source of love increases. In such a situation, it is not necessary to work in the event horizon. It is necessary to give current events a rest. The whole load should go to the field of ego stabilisation through social fulfilment, through social contacts and self-assertion in that field of life in which it is ecological—sports, routines, business, achievements, finances, projects and plans.

All of these aspects are very important for high self-esteem. The ego, finding itself in the world of people, does not create a field of tension at home, and home is truly free for love.

One case study on this topic is based on the story of Igor and Elena. Igor was like an explosive machine; all the time with strained nerves, periodic emotional breakdowns, alcohol abuse, and endless domestic grievances. Critical outbursts, raising his voice, the pressure, the demand for discipline, control over the household life of housemates—all this was as familiar a picture as the arrival of a new day on the calendar.

The issue from which so much resistance grew lay not in the realm of relationships, but in Igor's 'overheated' ego. The man was receiving a great deal of energy from his wife in the form of intimacy, loyalty, attention, belonging, but this energy was not finding an outlet in the necessary volume of social fulfilment, it was stagnating and turning into an aggressive swamp.

The ego, fuelled by feelings, strength, attention, was squeezed into its own frames and collapsed on loved ones like a rain of stones.

Igor had two choices.

To destroy his consciousness by the force of the explosion of his ego, which one day would overheat and ignite in a fit of asocial final act of self-destruction, which, of course, would end in loneliness, divorce, isolation, and a search for guilt for the rest of his life. Another way out is through the chronic deterioration of affairs, health, through separation from society to accept the signs that the path has gone the wrong way.

Our relatives were not given to us for domestic convenience, to feed our inner animals and to indulge our style of degradation. They are given as representatives of the Creator and his will, without whose presence the path to finding the integrity of one's consciousness is simply impossible.

Under these circumstances, only Igor, one out of 100, would revise his values on his own. For the other 99, a harsh karmic shake-up, loss of habitual way of life, and some kind of punishment are needed. On the brink of an abyss or in the face of death, one might want to question what exactly is wrong with one's behaviour, rather than with life in general.

In our story, Igor went fishing with friends, where he nearly drowned. He was soaked in water, dirty, exhausted, with a sunken stomach and red face, he lay on the ground and felt unspeakable anger, mixed with despair, loneliness, pain, and self-pity. Unable to bear these feelings, he burst into tears, then packed up his dirty things and went home.

At home, he kept quiet for six months and renovated the flat. And then it turned out that he wanted to build a house and make all of his wife's dreams come true in that house. And so their new life began.

Nature has put in human the desire to achieve goals related to their needs. If they achieve them, they feel satisfaction, joy, pleasure; this is their reward for success in matters important to nature. If goals are not achieved, they feel discomfort, dissatisfaction, physical and mental pain.

Something or someone we have to look for in life, for example, a suitable partner for a serious relationship. And with something we have to work, for example, with the same partner that we found, with whom we tied our fate, seeing in them the virtues important to us. But in spite of that, they will never be perfect, no matter how much we would like them to be.

So we should try to build a relationship with them in such a way that it is comfortable for both of us, giving in somewhere, agreeing somewhere, and respecting our interests—this is the construction of happiness. Relationships are work; they will never be that perfect so you can just enjoy them without having any problems.

People don't consider them seriously enough; they rely only on their feelings in this matter, completely without analysing the situation and the personality of their partner. They don't think about the prospects of a relationship with them, they don't even think about the reasons for their sympathy for them. They feel good and that's enough to consider their feelings serious.

They even talk about love, although what kind of love can there be in an immature relationship? And, if a person is not used to working on themselves, on the relationship, is not used to negotiate with their partner, to solve problems together, then it is easier for them to run away from these problems to another person, with whom at first it will be just as easy and interesting.

This is how one can run all their life and not come to anything. People believe that somewhere out there is the perfect partner for them, who only needs to be found. They don't think about their shortcomings, which can cause them problems in society, and they aren't going to work on them in order to correct them and increase their own value. No, they are looking for the easiest way: to avoid hardship by simply shifting from everything bad to everything supposedly good.

To deserve happiness is to attain to it. If this does not happen, happiness will be simple and temporary, not as serious and comprehensive as that of understanding, adult and responsible people who know the value of life's many important things.

Sometimes you just have to accept happiness when someone gives it to you, rather than neglecting it by being perpetually dissatisfied and displeased with everything. In that sense, it's not hard to deserve happiness if you're wise and know the measure of everything, otherwise it will always elude you.

Selfishness helps people to gain something that makes them temporarily happy, but it also forces them to lose a lot, sometimes much more than they gained through it. Therefore, the lot of the selfish person is loneliness and suffering associated with it. Not all lonely people are selfish, but almost all selfish people end up in loneliness, which is hell for a person. They stay with the one they have always truly loved: themselves.

The ego is useful and necessary, even though it sometimes looks unsightly. The problem is not the ego, but the fact that, apart from the ego, there is nothing.

The ego is formed to take, not to give. The ego saves, not gives. Giving is dealt with only by the personality. Therefore, in giving we put a barrier to the ego's manifestation, by generosity we limit it.

However, the ego knows how to find its benefit even in generosity. If a person gives themselves to someone (their energy, time, money), they may do it because their ego dictates so—for profit, for a pleasant feeling of inner satisfaction, because of a desire to show off in front of others...Real generosity is aimed at the other and their benefit, not at me and my profit. In everything that is directed at me, there is my ego.

The diseased ego is adaptive and adept at finding ways to remain the protagonist even when (especially when!) all one's energies are thrown into fighting it. Working with the ego is the most difficult part of self-improvement precisely because it is a necessary part of the individual.

The individual is not reduced to their ego. You cannot force yourself to work with your ego on its level. You can't work with the ego with its toolkit. One cannot concentrate on the ego, in any way, shape, or form. One must not concentrate even on eradicating it.

If you are familiar with the language of ascetics, think of pride. Pride is a sin that is not a transgression or an act; it is a condition. It is an ego that has captivated and filled a person.

But sin is not dealt with by negotiation, careful analysis, and scrutiny; it is eradicated by virtue, that is, by moving upward.

Don't try to tame the ego, better take care of yourself, your development, make yourself higher and bigger than your ego.

The ego must be healthy and, at the same time, nurtured. It should help a person in maintaining their identity, not dictate its will.

Do you want to defeat the ego? Depreciate it through the elevation of your personality. Prove to yourself that there is something else in you besides ego, above all spirituality.

You can start small by showing kindness, unselfishness, and love in your daily life, thereby getting closer to our true nature, regardless of what the rational mind tries to dictate.

God, grant us the grace to accept with serenity
That which cannot be changed,
The courage to change what can be changed,
And wisdom to distinguish one from the other.
Living each day to the fullest,
Rejoicing in every moment,
Accepting hardship as the path that leads to peace,
Accepting, just as Jesus accepted
This sinful world as it is,
And not as I would have it to be,
Trusting that Thou wilt make it all right,
If I submit myself to Thy will:
That I may acquire, within reasonable limits, happiness in this life,

And surpassing happiness with Thee forever and ever in the life to come.[9]

---

9 Karl Paul Reinhold Niebuhr (Karl Paul Reinhold Niebuhr; 1892–1971) was an American Protestant theologian of German origin.

Working with the Heart Centre of Consciousness

Let's discuss a very important topic—the work of the heart centre of consciousness[10], directly connected with love. There

---

10 Anahata-chakra is an energy-informational and energy centre that sublimates all kinds of energy received by a human being—an open biological system constantly exchanging various kinds of energy with the objects of the surrounding world. When, interacting with others, one is attuned to benevolence, sincerity, and compassion, one gets an opportunity to develop the full potential of anahata-chakra.

Through this centre, the nature of the individual soul and of God is manifested. Human is the only living being of the material world capable not only of experiencing but also of cultivating love.

Anahata is the soil on which the seeds of love are planted. Here, you can grow a whole garden, which will give wonderful fruit, bringing joy and happiness to those around you. Hypocrisy, fear, self-interest, hatred, and indifference do not allow the lotus of anahata-chakra to open and the energy of love, which is the essence of our spiritual nature, to manifest.

Unfortunately, in this age, people communicate with each other on a very low, heartless level. They do not perceive those around them are no people for whom life without love would be attractive. If it were announced to all of us tomorrow that we would henceforth live as rational beings without a sense of love, many of us would want to leave this planet. But if love is so important to us, then why do we encounter it so rarely and briefly?

Why is it fleeting? Why are the most successful, strongest, truest, most sparkling marriages most often just partnerships?

Romance writers claim that love lives for three years. We experience different kinds of love: erotic, sexual, soulful, creative. Love for a child, self-sacrificing love. We can't live without all of these things, but how do we attract all of them and build a relationship with our love?

Open your hearts, remember your own love stories.

Do you think love is driven by people?

Do you think that Cupid, Psyche, Aphrodite generate it? That they spread love among us mortals?

Yes, we feel jealous of those who have the happiness of love. We care a great deal that someone else has it in their life. At our best, we begin to realise that life itself is the road to love.

Having met it, we very often find ourselves unable to understand what its space should be, what the quality of dialogue with it should be. And in general, how to properly

---

as individuals, so communication is often filled with lies, pride, indifference, hypocrisy, envy, and malice.

The beginning of the relationship between a man and a woman is often based only on passion; connection through the heart is lost. Later, they will create a family in which there is no love. The children born to them will be deprived of this divine energy from an early age, and there will be a 'father–child problem'.

and harmoniously utilise it, so that love becomes the river of our happiness.

At one of our training sessions, we studied the principles of interpersonal relationships. Half of the attendees declared their deep monogamy, forming relationships with one person. The other half (mostly men) insisted exclusively on polygamy. Naturally, as usual, there was a small, angry group of intellectuals (the author was among them) who declared serial monogamy.

Everyone liked this definition so much that several people from the polygamy and monogamy camps, realising that they liked it better, changed the flag. As a result, the group of angry intellectuals became the largest.

The concept of serial monogamy tells you that you are completely faithful and committed to whomever you are with at the moment. This is the first law of the tantric relationship: to be, above all, close to yourself, and to experience the feeling of love at every moment, because in the eyes of the other, you ultimately meet yourself.

Love is a collective image of God, who has many hypostases. He is beautiful, terrible, bold, and wise. He is a creator, unfathomable in His greatness and diversity. And Love is like Him.

In feeling and accepting another person's soul, we take the first step in great knowledge. Accepting their body, we take the next step. We accept their behaviour, their manner of speaking, their mistakes, their sufferings, their weaknesses, taking countless steps, accepting and uniting more and more faces of creation into one.

On the contrary, in pushing something away, we lose integrity.

How many rays does the sun have? How many angels are in heaven? How many faces does God have?

Imagine that the sun warms you with all its rays, and you get picky and start deciding which ones can touch your skin and which ones can't. It's the same with love. It is only when we remove the barriers of accepting absolutely all the faces of God that we experience a state of absolute, divine, infinite love. For some it is spiritual, for some it is tantric, for some it is something else. All rays shine upon us.

If we reject some of them, love punishes us. Deep down, we are often afraid of its appearance, because we know that it can be painful.

I'm not talking about clinical cases of co-dependency, where non-adult parts of the psyche enter into a loving relationship and, in doing so, our inner little children seek out daddy and mommy. It's not about opening up the heart centre of consciousness either; it's about a spiritual motherhood program where we learn to share ourselves within the family, and the theme of needing, caring within the family.

But here's the situation. Five years of being together and the woman says, "That's it, I don't want it anymore. Yes, we have children. So what? I'm leaving, let him manage on his own."

But you created him and this reality. And now, instead of accepting everything and trying to open your heart to all the hypostases of the divine principle as a state of love, and to assemble a holistic image, you come to denial.

All that you have known, knows you, too, it is always with you, it always finds you. For example, this is the image of the Creator in the person of a man who creates some extraordinary objects of art. They surround you, become you and your world that you love. But if your heart is closed because you do not accept some faces of God, they will seem unnecessary, ugly.

The heart, no matter how much sex you offer it, says, "I'll certainly wait until you get everything you want: a man, a woman, their bodies, their moods. They'll probably even get married formally. But that's not what I want. It doesn't penetrate into me at all, and I crave other things. I am your only organ that can accommodate not just knowledge and perceptions, but the energy of God and the whole world."

The price of our life is equal to our ability, through the heart, to contain the whole world, and to become that world.

The heart is like an airport, the soul is like an aeroplane, the spirit is like a pilot. If the heart is closed and the soul has nowhere to land, it cannot give us talents, abilities and opportunities for fulfilment.

Often we look for Hollywood plots in life. Here we meet a man who seems to have gone all the way, who has absorbed all the faces of God. His heart is open, and he is about to meet us and give us everything. But he may have known and let into himself the countenance of the Virgin Mary, without which it is impossible to be a civilised man, and, for example, also the image of erotic perfection.

And we begin to demand from the man: show us the faces of the God of love. Where is all love at all? And the man cannot, because in fact he is also still learning and searching. And it is good, if he is searching at all.

But let's go back to the beginning and remember that in any science, there is a concept of subject-object. In our context, the object is a man, and the subject is the face of God. What can we call the face of God and what can we not? How do we know: are we dealing with something simply good and beautiful, or are we dealing with the countenance of God in something?

For example, we find ourselves in the countryside. A field, a river, a forest, the sky. There is the face of God in all of that. And here we are looking at a very realistic, gorgeous photo wallpaper. There's a field, a river, a forest, the sky. But there's no face of God there. And it's impossible to be deceived, impossible to confuse.

The human heart is alive, to the extent that they are aware of these images of God inside themselves. To the extent that they are in a dialogue with them, how many of them they have in their heart. If they have only 'give me' in heart, it's a different story. Attention and love, energy and care, the right attitude and support, belonging and intimacy…give me all of that.

Such a heart, as if turned inside out, feels cut open, gutted. It is unable to fill up, no matter how much it draws in, how much it absorbs. For the more it takes in, the more is taken out. And all that is left is disappointment, pain, resentment.

Love is all the faces of God on the planet, and a person has as many faces of love in their heart as they can hold.

At my counselling session, one girl told me how she fell in love with a man and sent him her love. She imagined an image of him, telling him of the enormous feeling of love she was sending him on a daily basis. She had no doubt that she was literally bathing her chosen one in the energy of her heart. In reality, she had simply raised his astral double and overfed him with her energy.

How can we truly synchronise with our loved ones?

For someone, the sunset over the sea is an open state of love to God and a man, who also perceives the sunset in an open state of love. And a common language of love is formed that is absolutely universal and in which there can be no difference of opinion. There will never be an argument about whether this sunset is bad or good. Simply, he and she will become bathed in love for that sunset.

And if one lacks these faces of God, and has a very scarce language of love, then the perception of the world shifts to the lower energy centres (svadhisthana).

Here it is necessary to make some digression and remind what svadhisthana and other chakras are, what they represent.

The dense and subtle bodies of humans are connected to the universe by countless nadhi channels belonging not to the 'dense' but to the 'subtle' body and uniting the so-called chakras—special zones of both the 'dense' and 'subtle' bodies. On the subtle plane, the chakras are associated with the primary elements of the universe—the elements of 'earth', 'fire', 'water', 'air', and 'ether'. The seven main chakras are located on the central line of the body.

The chakras have the ability to accumulate and transform certain types of energies used by the body for various purposes. Resembling rotating spheres, they are attuned to the appropriate frequency resonances of the micro- and macrocosm.

Muladhara-chakra, which projects in the area of the perineum between the anus and the external genitals, is one of the most important energy structures of the body. It is here that the irreplaceable energy of the body, called ojas (the Chinese call it yuan-qi), is 'stored'. We receive ojas at conception and use it actively only during the period of intrauterine development and growth.

As long as a person does not deplete his or her ojas, he or she is not in danger of old age, multiple diseases, or death. Ojas is the basis of immunity and homeostasis (constancy of the internal environment), as well as our natural biological clock. People dominated by muladhara-chakra have extraordinary physical strength and stamina, but are usually not well-developed spiritually or intellectually.

They live mainly by selfish interests, are prone to hoarding (even of things they do not really need), and take little interest in the problems of others. Lacking imagination and creativity, they willingly do the same uncomplicated work that does not require much ingenuity (e.g., on an assembly line). They can eat any food, even badly cooked and spoiled, and they rarely get sick.

They are inert, are in a half-asleep state even during the day, do not experience strong feelings. It can be said that they are not quite aware of the reality around them.

Svadhisthana-chakra is the centre of accumulation and transmutation of shakti energy (sometimes it is called sexual energy), which, similar to water, can assume three aggregative states: to accumulate in muladhara-chakra (solid), to be used in sexual intercourse (liquid), or to be transformed into creative potential (gaseous). Svadhisthana-chakra projects in the area of IV–V lumbar vertebrae and extends its influence mainly to the organs of the pelvis and kidneys.

People in whom the influence of this chakra predominates live primarily by emotions. They believe in and seek only that which they can directly see, touch, or taste. Very impressionable and changeable in mood, they do not use logic and awareness of the world around them. More often they live for a day, blow with the wind.

They are characterised by superstitions. They are subject to a 'herd mentality'. They are utterly impractical, but very sensitive. They have a great attachment to sexual pleasures and are very prolific.

Manipura-chakra, which transforms and stores energy from digestion and breathing, is localised in the solar plexus.

Those with a dominant Manipura-chakra influence are incredibly active. They are constantly in the whirlpool of events. However, their actions are very chaotic, and their efforts do not correspond to the results obtained. They are very strongly attached to the objects of the feelings.

They are not satisfied only with food, sleep and sexual pleasures. They crave power, strength, wealth, honours, fame, and for this they spend a tremendous amount of energy. Their whole life is a long-distance run. They have no time to think about the essence of existence. They are characterised by self-centredness, pride, and arrogance. They are quite inordinate in sensual pleasures, though they try to make them as refined as possible.

Anahata-chakra is projected in the area of V–VI thoracic vertebrae, slightly to the right of the sternum.

People with a predominant influence of the anahata-chakra have an open heart. They are very sincere and simple in their behaviour. An extraordinary warmth of spirit comes from them. They are kind and merciful, they respect others and always try to help those in need. They are benevolent and treat everybody equally regardless of age and social status. In personal life, they are satisfied with little.

Very hardworking, like creativity, they put their heart and soul into everything they do. They usually tell the truth to others, but try not to hurt their feelings. In religious practices, they often go the way of bhakti (development of a personal relationship with God on the basis of friendship and love). God and all the celestial hierarchs are very favourable to such people, even if they are not very developed spiritually and do not have much intelligence.

Vishuddha-chakra is projected in the thyroid area. It is connected with the senses and subcortical areas of the brain on the one hand, and with the mental body on the other.

Those who have a predominant influence of vishuddha-chakra have high creative abilities. They are people of the arts—musicians, painters, sculptors, poets, and actors. They have an excellent command of their voice and have the ability to convey any information, converting it into an appropriate form. They can engage in various crafts that require creative and unconventional approach, and they cannot stand standards and monotonous activities.

The ajna-chakra, projected in the area between the eyebrows, transforms and accumulates energy, which contributes to the process of logical thinking (active analysis and synthesis of information). This centre ensures the functioning of the cells of the cerebral cortex, which is the receiving device of the human intellectual body.

Ajna-chakra receives energy through the subtle body and transforms the kinetic energy of the manipura, and in case of great mental exertion, also of the svadhisthana. Some of this energy can be sublimated and used by the lower chakras. In other words, the process of thinking is also a source of energy for the body—thus, many scientists feel a great burst of energy during active thought work.

People with the dominant influence of the ajna-chakra have well-developed intellect and logical thinking. They are most interested in knowledge in life. There are many scientists and philosophers among them. They explore all manifestations of life, have developed thinking, but their sensitivity and intuition, as a rule, are poorly developed because they believe only in what can be confirmed by experiment or physical examination.

Some of them, however, become sages when they learn the truth. Their faith is usually based on their own experience, knowledge, and observation of the world around them. Spiritually, they usually choose the path of gyana (cultivating spiritual knowledge with a gradual understanding of their original position in relation to God and the laws of the universe). They usually avoid a personal relationship with God, perceiving Him as the Absolute Truth.

Sahasrara-chakra, which projects at the junction of the occipital and two parietal bones (the opening of the great fontanelle), refers to the so-called 'aggregor centre'. Becoming a follower of a certain spiritual-religious tradition, a person immediately receives support and protection of the corresponding aggregor. Abstract thinking, creativity, meditation and clairvoyance are connected with functioning of the sahasrara-chakra.

Contact with higher forces of nature is impossible without its opening. If this centre is blocked, one is deprived of support from above. Descending stream movement is disturbed, a person becomes too earthy, the sphere of their interests is strongly narrowed. They lose their memory, and sometimes their mind.

People with the predominant influence of sahasrara-chakra are rare in this world. They are always outstanding personalities, conductors of different aggregors. L. N. Gumilev called them passionaries. They have a strong influence on the course of history, they are given the ability to invigorate and inspire others, they are followed by hundreds and thousands.

Some of them, consciously or not, perform the tasks of the celestial hierarchy, so they can receive unlimited opportunities. Be they even evil geniuses, until they fulfil their mission, no one can do anything to them. They are under strong protection, their life and destiny do not belong to them. Some of them are guides to the will of God, and then they are called prophets and saints. These men can work miracles because they are given power and energy from on high.

Our heart works according to how many images are within us, whether they have become part of us, and whether we have committed our heart to love this world. And have we given ourselves completely to it.

If we are on the human side of reality, and we only have a human idea of love and family and relationships, then we will actually just get a family all the time. And family is responsibilities. There is no such thing as a family outside of responsibilities. A family stands on three pillars. When all three of these pillars are healthy and harmonious, one builds an ideal family with an ideal relationship.

First pillar: You have to work on your very self and make the family happy.

Second pillar: You have to work on yourself and make the family happy.

The third pillar: You have to work on yourself as well as make your family happy.

Period.

It often occurs to people who seem to have achieved family harmony, that they do not feel that harmony. They do not feel that this gift is present. But it is not a gift; it is the sacred work of the heart centre within us.

It is necessary to let the face of God inside us, symbolising forgiveness. If your heart is a precious diamond, look for what it will resonate with so that it can forgive.

On top of personal relationships, you need to make a spiritual path to the face of God associated with acceptance. These are the states where people who have been through some very difficult experiences understand exactly what stands between them. And when they realise that there is an understanding of forgiveness. It doesn't mean that they forget about the war that once existed between them. It means that they choose the path to peace.

With forgiveness, it will be easier for the heart to know love, to find that special person who is really right for you.

With forgiveness comes kindness in the heart. If this kindness becomes the face of God, it can be called unconditional ethics. This divine countenance, associated with an absolute ethics of values, gives one a perfectly clear understanding of whether something is ethical or unethical on a spiritual level

Such a person will never cross the ethics of divine law with their heart. They will be ready to lose even their body, but to preserve the state of absolute balance and the true value of all things. And in this aspect you can get close to a person as much as you like, because it will be love.

There are so many important things that have to do with making the presence of God within the heart conscious. In one of the trainings, I asked the participants to draw their hearts and any three symbols that were present either inside or next to the heart. The drawing was done spontaneously, without thinking. Everyone depicted their hearts in different ways.

There, for example, was a heart that had no boundaries. The man simply placed himself in the centre of the world. This means that one of his parents was good and did not cause the child terrible trauma. Because the heart only becomes that way when at least one of the parents had tremendous, unconditional love for the child.

And there was a dialogue with a heart through the prism of a certain pattern that symbolises eroticism. This means that you, somewhere deep inside, are attached to the perception of love through eroticism, which you have formed at a subconscious level.

And there's a story about a man with infinity in his heart.

And what does the burning flame inside the heart symbolise, what is the face of God? When God manifests himself in this way, how do we feel? Such a flame is a symbol that one's heart, life and soul become in the highest sense a sacrifice to the Most High.

And on this fire, the Self and the Ego are burned, personal limitations are burned, and you burn and give yourself to the world. This pleasure is unspeakable. It changes the picture of the world; it changes life; it changes reality and your body, which begins to heal.

The heart has so much energy, it can heal your illnesses. Everything that has to do with self-healing, with healing, has to do with the heart. That's why it's important to listen to your heart, to open up to it, and to live in contact with it. It can give you with great love a completely different physical well-being, both spiritually and morally.

The heart is the mirror of the world, reflecting the whole universe.

The Words of Sufi Jalal ad-Din Loras.

Our heart is bigger than the universe. We are by no means small on the scale of Creation. Moreover, we are the reason creation took place at all. And no angels, prophets, or teachers can be an obstacle between us and God. God created us so that we could connect with Him. God said: "I created people, who are higher than many, many angels. People are my representatives." We are all God's representatives when we live on earth.

We are much larger than the universe, though we don't even know its true size yet. Our inner ocean is much larger than the earth's ocean. And, if we are able to enter our ocean with God's grace, our ecstasy begins, and love is increasing. We see no imperfections, because God makes everything perfect. We can reach that level ourselves, and help those around us. Trust yourself. God is always with you.

Open your hearts. We are here to learn and teach at the same time. You have many treasures. Be generous, share them.

Generosity is not about taking out your wallet and giving away your money. Generosity comes in many ways. To look at someone and say, 'You are beautiful' is generosity. We can see beauty everywhere—in children, in animals, in a flower.

We admire the beauty of any of God's creations, and that is generosity.

Every morning, we wake up and look in the mirror. Are we generous enough to kiss ourselves, our reflection in the mirror, and say, "Thank you, Creator, for creating such a beautiful being. Please help me to open my heart to You." Asking God for help is also generosity.

Each of us came from God's first kiss, by which He brought His light into a man. This is why we love kisses. And it's not just us. Even animals, when showing love, kiss. It's not necessarily the same kiss as ours, but there are many different ways to kiss.

God originally does everything for us, but we are not aware of it. We think, we do, we say, we love and we are angry, being a part of Him. But would He put Himself in hell, burn Himself there? No.

And we all come from heaven, too. We all have a palace in heaven with a golden throne. Each of us is a king and a queen in the kingdom of heaven. We belong to heaven, and we are here in this world for a little while. Here we cry, we are sad, but when we return to heaven, we become happy, because we are greeted and welcomed there with a pure heart.

Part II
We are Partners

Each of us is looking for an understanding of exactly what constitutes a relationship in our lives. What is a true partnership and what is not. And how we come to script the right relationship.

All relationships in our lives, in one way or another, come in three types.

The First Type of Relationship.

These are karmic relationships with our partners that we met in a past life, and inevitably meet in this one. Tarot cards, numerology, western and eastern astrology show, calculate when a karmic partner will appear. A good half of all relationships are with karmic partners, and are usually for paying off some kind of karmic debt.

But whenever we meet a karmic partner, these debts throw our consciousness off from the objective reality. That is, we are traumatised as a result of having to behave in one way or another, but we cannot avoid these karmic relationships, which, for example, may be between parents and children.

Karmic relationships are not meant to evolve, and that is their danger.

We cannot develop radically new strategies of behaviour because we have certain commitments from the past, and this distorts and breaks the sense of our own possibilities in relationships. We begin to create certain self-esteem patterns for ourselves, to draw certain, far-reaching conclusions that are usually unfounded.

It is impossible to analyse what we are like in a relationship, and what kind of relationship suits us, based on the experience of a karmic relationship. Karmic relationships are not given for us to develop, to conceptualise our relationships with other people. They are not given for us to experience happiness in them.

This is the negative experience that prevents us from realising our own great possibilities, our own uniqueness in building relationships.

The Second Type of Relationship.

These relationships are creative, project-based—the ones that our very nature, evolution itself connects us to those around us.

Identical development, similar qualities, pursuit of the same goals. Just as a grain of sand is attracted to other grains to form a mountain, just as several trees form a grove, we are attracted to each other based on the functional, objective needs of world evolution. Our encounters and interactions generate a creative environment, creative aspirations, new perspectives on development.

It is a functional-project relationship that emerges from the possibilities of social development and the capacities of the individual. Anyone who has been in such a relationship begins to see the broadest horizon of possibilities. 'My God, I can do this and that! I have so many talents!'. And it turns out that relationships can be managed and, thanks to that, they can change the world, create and accumulate something.

So if in karmic relationships we basically 'clean up the old rubble' and we can't access any creativity, then it's completely different with project-functional relationships. It is not created by karma but the evolution, which requires different principles of alignment, different communication, different system of sharing values, different goalsetting.

People very often do not understand who is in front of them and may be frightened of a project-functional partner. After all, they think that something incredibly difficult for them is about to begin; not only that, they may be challenged in some karmic way. And on the contrary, very often they try to make a project out of a karmic relationship. That is they want to save it, change it, build something good. But karmic relationships are only amenable to healing in life.

If you make too many mistakes while creating a project relationship, it may very quickly turn into a karmic one. Where freedom, spaciousness and independence reigned, people out of habit begin to build unnecessary models, and thus close for themselves the next stage of evolution, which the relationship with this or that person embodied.

The Third Type of Relationship.

These are relationships that are given to us with a purpose of living the higher mental functions (including love and those aspects that form the experience of our soul), for expanding our worldview. When such people appear in our lives, our hearts open up through them, amazing new horizons of worldview are born. Through these people comes a radically new reading of destiny and what we call love in the spiritual, psychological sense.

When a person comes to you, to your space, it is very important to feel and understand what type of relationship he or she carries.

But is it possible to live all three scenarios simultaneously with the same person?

It is possible, but with such a person, you need to live your whole life in fidelity in order to transit from karma to building something else, and as a result of this building to give birth to a true feeling of love. Not infatuation, not passion. Love is a very pure, magical source that never opens by itself.

Astrologers know the wonderful White Moon, Selene. She measures the life of a couple by seven years. In the first seven years, she gives a lot of resources to make a couple. The second seven years, she tests the couple. After fourteen years, if the couple passes their integrity exams, they go on to twenty-one years and then become a true couple. Selene gives, in this case, the cosmic unity of souls, the rapprochement and the absolute union of man and woman.

Classical western astrology helps us to understand how the stars regulate our lives and how to meet someone with whom we can live out all three types of relationships. Very rarely do we meet such a 'person of destiny', and yet some of us have karma signs pointing to just one partner with whom we go hand in hand all our lives.

It seems wonderful and incredibly inspiring at first. But the reality of being begins, and one comes to understand what it's like in practice. With only one person. Without the right to make a mistake. All the way to old age.

And some people say, "No, it's a good thing I don't have that fate. I'd rather work this out with one person and that with another, and with a third, some other layer of relationship."

A true partnership is precisely a project relationship. A project can be a joint business, building a family, and having a child. A project can be anything that has to do with creating something on the basis of shared resources in order to achieve any positive results. As mentioned, in a karmic relationship you cannot build a project, you can only heal the system you exist in.

If you choose a relationship with a karmic partner, you will be healing for twenty-one years, in essence, the structure of the kin and the structure of the relationship within it. Often such couples are surprised that they cannot reach a decent level of income, have children, build a house, achieve any results. But they love each other and want to continue to be together.

Such couple has a karmic marriage, and consequently, there are so many internal, psychological, emotional tasks that it is simply impossible to quickly implement any project.

Horoscopes show in which sphere you will have more karmic partners and where there are complicated aspects. This could be work, creativity, spirituality, family, love relationships.

Love and family relationships are controlled by different sectors in astrology, so you clearly see where you have burdens, and you understand that you will have partners burdened by karma in that segment. But arising complexities are functional and connected with the development of systems, so they are not an absolute barrier for creative self-actualisation.

If you are burdened by karma in the field of career and self-realisation, then difficult employers, difficult subordinates, difficult creditors, difficult landlords, i.e., all those with whom you have to build professional communications, will flow through your life. And managing your relationships in life is a very important thing because it helps you decide on the most important resource in life of human connections.

Social connections cost a lot, and this is a very important project for every person. Who do I connect with? How do I connect? Who is around me? It is very important to identify your risk areas. It's very important to understand where in life there the greatest likelihood of meeting teachers is.

I call karmic partners our teachers because when they appear in our sight, we are irresistibly attracted to them; we can do nothing with ourselves, we start to build relationships that end or sometimes last with very great complications for us. If you understand that the goal is to heal, not to get a relationship format, it's certainly a great relief for the psyche.

True, there is no chance to build something constructive, but there is a chance to heal something here and there, to change a lot of things in the value system and to align the overall way of how life resources are exchanged.

If a karmic person calls me on the phone, then I try to be a karmic guide myself, take the initiative, take the responsibility, prepare myself for these calls, knowing already everything that is waiting for me. I try to call them myself, because when they call me, it's like the space police control.

And in talking to you, they'll twist things up in the worst way possible for you. You are enjoying being in some wonderful place, but a karmic person calls, and your state of enchantment immediately evaporates. These people in general have a great power over our moods, our behaviour, our feelings.

On the contrary, with creative people you can make money, build connections, make some unexpected, unordinary decisions.

Think of your immediate environment. Without overthinking, spontaneously, choose from it 10–15 people. For example, this would be your husband and wife, your brother and sister, your uncle and aunt, your employees. Divide them in three columns according to the type of relationship.

With those in the karmic relationship column, your job is to always be focused on improving situations. As you heal these relations, step by step they will start to become more harmonious, more transparent, more understandable, more adequate. Because this sector of your relations is a hole in which a lot of energy, information, resources disappear.

Generally, in the karmic relationship it is very difficult to understand how, why, who owes what to whom. And it's very important to be focused on healing, no matter what's going on. Roughly speaking, karmic relationships are the result of our dark side bringing them into our lives to work out some shadowy aspects.

To heal means to add warmth, love, tenderness, gifts, attention no matter what. In the karmic group, the main style of communication is provocation. The person periodically provokes you to anything. To emotions that you did not want to experience, to feelings that are very difficult for you (perhaps, it is a financial relationship that you were not prepared for).

There is a certain cycle of working off karmic relationships, and if it's a marital relationship, then the first fourteen years are karma in its purest form. Then people are rebuilding for another seven years, and if they've been together for twenty-one years and retained intimacy, then they're already out of the karmic zone of the relationship.

Correspondingly, there are certain stages when you may feel that karma with this person is over for you, you've healed it.

If we look at creative-functional relationships, how do we recognise such people? They present us with a certain challenge, a certain bar to which we need to grow with that person.

With the first column, you have to be tolerant and teach yourself to be patient, to be quiet, to stomach and give warmth, and with the second column, you have to constantly push yourself to do something. In front of you is a challenge to your ambitions, your hopes, your desires. And so, these people, their energy opens up the possibility of consolidation and constructive communication.

This is the relationship of partnership, a social one, and implementing our social program. They are determined by our development, by our freedom in the world of people, in the evolutionary community—inter-human, professional, spiritual. Where there are few social relationships, there will be a lack of creative fulfilment of one's life ambitions.

But not all relationships in life are true partnerships. Let's say a man of blessing comes to you, bringing the message of love. What kind of partner is he to you? He is pure happiness. The relationship with him will be built in a system of completely different values—just happiness, absolute love.

How do you know if someone is a blessing to you? When people come from this sector, they bring forgiveness. Suddenly, there is a boss with whom you have the same thoughts and feelings. He is willing to give you interest-free corporate loans and send you on business trips abroad. He builds for you absolute support, absolute purity of space.

These are people of blessing, and it is very important not to confuse them with others. They come from other spaces to bring you love, a reference point, a beacon. A meeting with such people always brings new hope, a kind of inspiration, and even salvation. You draw from such relationships the ability to love unconditionally; you draw contact with your soul and the experience of opening yourself fully to the world. A light relationship is a gift from God.

Sometimes, when we rashly and recklessly build a relationship with someone from the first group, we hope that the feelings will be the same as those from the last group. No, this is an illusion. This can happen after the karmic program is over and people haven't really gotten tired of each other yet and decided to stay together.

The more karmic relationships a person has in their life, the harder it is for them to fill in the other two groups.

It's very important to make sure that you don't get stuck in a karmic relationship, depriving yourself of the opportunity to let partners into your life who come only for love, and who are like guardian angels to you.

But back to the middle column (true partnership). These people are characterised by the fact that they are always complementary, that is, you complement each other on opposite qualities. True partners are those people who complement you. Which sector do you think is the most successful way to start a family?

The middle one. The most successful marriages that lead to evolution, abundance and prosperity are here because, in a good way, these are marriages of positive interest, of positive gain, of complementarity.

Those who have severely traumatised relationships because of difficult karmic ties either with partners or with parents, dream of a soulmate and a marriage of love. But for evolution, for development, we do not need a soulmate, but someone who is complementary. That is, they haves qualities that are opposite, that complement you. This theory was scientifically proven by Jung, who identified four human psychotypes: extrovert, introvert, rational, and irrational.

Later, on the basis of this personality typology, the researcher Aušra Augustinavičiūtė developed the concept of duality[11] in socionics.

Duality has no scientific status, but social experiments within the framework of this concept have proven that complementary personalities work most effectively in a

---

11 The concept was first used by socionics founder Aušra Augustinavičiūtė in 1983 in her book *Human Dual Nature*, which argues that duality is vital for normal life, well-being and health, because in such a union, partners' strengths are fully and adequately realised and weaknesses are protected.

Dual relationship is one of the 16 types of intertype relationships described in socionics. Partners who are in a dual relationship are also called 'duals'.

Dual relationships are one of the main concepts of socionics and are characterised by mutual benefit and support, and are considered optimal for friendship, intimacy, and marriage (although sociotype is not the only factor determining the success of an interaction). They are considered the 'most important' relationships because they are a manifestation of psychological compatibility, and best for a multitude of interaction and communication situations: work, parenting, leisure, and business partnerships. A synonym for the term 'dual relationship' is 'full complementary relationship'.

union, while being quite close to each other spiritually and emotionally.

But, usually, we are not looking for a partner with whom we will create, work, and build, mutually complementing each other in creativity. No, we are looking for someone who has experienced emotional traumas of intimacy as a child, and who will understand and appreciate our own traumas. Will understand our souls, will share our pain, will be close to us to compensate for the traumas of the past.

But here's a positive example for you: the complementary marriage of Yana Rudkovskaya and Evgeni Plushenko. These are people with radically different life competencies, psychological models and motivational structures, completely different social backgrounds and professional history. But when they are complementary in tune, then a brilliant whole is created.

This does not mean that each is just half of the whole. It means that each is self-sufficient, healthy and whole, and when they connect, they cover all sectors of the functional capacities of the psyche.

This is more difficult for women to grasp than for men. You have to explain that your husband is rational, he wants to calculate everything, prove everything, plan everything for the long term. He's not inclined to read esoteric books with you, do your favourite meditations and card layouts. He doesn't understand you. But he doesn't have to understand you.

For the evolution and viability of the system, he has to learn your qualities from you, and you have to learn his qualities from him, and by starting this learning you will evolve and receive those competences that would be unavailable for you in another algorithm of events.

And then marriage begins to evolve. People learn from each other, they gain qualities they have lacked, and they take the exciting path of constantly learning something new. They stop expecting to be accepted as they are. If the dominant idea is that "he will always be with me in intimacy, empathetic and understanding and sharing my path," this is not an evolutionary concept. It is a flawed approach to relationship building.

A complete match of souls, with two eyes for two and one heart for two, is possible in the third segment, but it is where social partnership becomes irrelevant. Think of the Master and Margarita. When they came together in mutual understanding, they combined worldviews and did not rush to write books, have children, or open stores. They became participants in a story that had nothing to do with society.

Yes, in the third version, people can build a family and a relationship, but it will be a rather closed, specific space. That's what the Roerichs were, for example. With the Roerichs, family was possible because they had no karmic relationships with their parents. When the father and mother are not karmic, then your consciousness is pure, you can build a family that is outside of society.

If the mother and father are from a karmic history and you meet a great love, what do you think will outweigh? The father and the mother. If you are held within a social relationship by karmic ties, you will not be able to build a family with that person.

You will experience some amazing story, get in touch with God within your partner, and yet you will find yourself held captive by karma, which will force you to return to its plot.

The film *The Nameless Star* tells such a story. This intricacy of karmic and spiritual relationships is the maze within which we move. And, one of the skills of getting the relationship right is not to confuse one with the other, to negotiate your destiny correctly.

And if you stop fulfilling karmic obligations altogether, it will be difficult to carry out creative projects. Creative resources will dry up, it will be difficult to maintain relationships with people who are out of karma.

But of course, we dream of having a certain degree of freedom. To communicate as much as we want and with as many people as we want. After all, it is these kinds of contacts that fill us up with what we want. This is the great dream of one and all. And it's achievable if you put everything in its place.

You clearly understand that here are the debts, here are the prospects. And here you have to relax, trust, and feel that this is exactly the place where your soul can really be with itself. And you don't have to try to choose a result or heal some process or some person in this moment.

It also happens that people meet and feel a mutual romantic attraction. If they're in a karmic group, there's no choice, the marriage has to happen. And, even if they, after tearing themselves away from each other with flesh and blood, with losses and emotional trauma, don't get married, "it will be like that, there is no other way."

Yes, they will exclaim together, "Not me! It's a good thing I had the strength to break up. My intuition was screaming that there was going to be big problems...and I didn't get into them." Then what happens to this karma next? It comes in the form of the next partner with the same scenario. Instead of one karmic partner comes a second one exactly the same.

The string is endless if your karmic relationship sector is family and marriage, and they will all go under the banner of 'hard life'.

It is very difficult to heal this. Different spiritual traditions offer different tools for this. In India, for example, many sacrifices are made, a person prays for this area of life. There are Orthodox who are engaged in permanent purification of karma. Sometimes people resort to psychotherapy and remove karmic programs from their subconscious, thus speeding up the process of getting out of the karmic zone.

Of course, we learn relationships only in the zone of true partnership by meeting those with whom we are complementary. And, if we are lucky and our marriage, our immediate environment is from this area, then we really need to learn relationships through training, reading books, constantly learning new skills. After all, these relationships are going to need to evolve, to become more and more effective.

And if you realise that a creative project with this or that person does not correspond to the second type, but the other type, should you shut down this project due to its futility, or continue?

Yes, it happens when a person from the third group shows up with an offer of creative collaboration. When two co-founders create something, and their energy is enough to find people from the second sector. They will work on that energy because in the third segment a large energy field is formed when you come into contact with them. And then the creative process is fuelled by the power of organisational management.

But if the person with whom you have a certain joint project is of the first type, then what should you do: engage in joint creativity or sort out karmic rubble?

It all depends on what exactly you are doing. If it is a project that requires immediate 'resuscitation' and immediate ordering, karmic relationships can help. If it is a question of creating something and developing some dynamic system (getting clean money for funding, implementing a startup, establishing a venture capital fund or getting a loan from a bank), then karmic relationships will destroy everything.

They're good where you need to untangle knots and harness the energy of healing. For instance, the karmic relationship of Holmes and Watson, who are involved in detective stories all the time rather than setting up a publishing house, for example. And their constant internal collisions only amplify the transformational energy.

And there can be different systems of dealing not just with people but with some areas of life. And, if you are looking to create a creative aura, a karmic relationship is not suitable here because, in this case, you will be releasing energy in the couple that is contrary to the very idea.

Yes, it's very important to understand what kind of relationship you have. Astrology can help here, but who looks at a horoscope? A successful international investor, a housewife, a professional astrologer? They have very different views on relationships as a resource.

And besides, one has to understand, is the person in their right place? Perhaps they are so entangled in their own karma, in such a karmic relationship with themselves, that they shouldn't even think about a true partnership. Who are you—to yourself? This is also a very important point.

By the way, the sun and the moon in the horoscope answer this very question. Some people have a very good relationship with their destiny while others have the worst. And if you have created a tangled karmic relationship with yourself, and your life is nothing but overcoming, then first of all it makes sense to untangle this knot. Do this, so that there will be more creative resource in your own life and destiny.

After that, you can move on to relationships with other people, because to dive into this world, confused in yourself, is fraught with danger.

If a person, for example, has a cardinal opposition of the Moon and the Sun, it will show that their soul and spirit will always argue. This is inherently a huge karmic conflict with oneself, one of the hardest aspects in horoscopes. A person with moon and sun opposition needs the help of a therapist to maintain a balance of mental assets, to receive constant support and some kind of administration.

From a past life, they bring a state of deep confrontation with themselves or extraordinary baggage through which they can be their own enemy, friend or blessing.

But who are you to the other people with whom you interact? After all, not only do they represent a type to you, but you represent a type to them as well. Relationships are not symmetrical; they may not match. You may perceive a man as creative, you have no karmic departures in relation to him, while he has karmic departures in relation to you.

And if you need to understand what you are to another person, ask him/her quickly, spontaneously, to fill in the table I was telling you about.

If you are an element of karma for them, let them serve you, work out their karmic debt for you. This is a system of subordinate-leader. For example, the husband has money, and the wife has no money. She has karmic aspects to her husband, he has no karmic aspects to her. She, in fact, considers him an oppressor, and he creates the conditions of working off debts to him.

But how do you build a successful business with someone who is in the third sector for you?

A great example is the Hewlett-Packard Corporation. Its founders, who loved each other, enthusiastically worked together on engines, soldering and drilling something. But for a corporation to be born, it needed a healthy board of founders who could manage the strategy, see the future, and navigate the market.

In order for the relationship to become the second type, one should not pile on each other's debts and obligations, should not take the happiness of a free relationship for granted, should not take advantage of each other. Don't try to formalise everything very rigidly because there is a lot of freedom in this relationship.

Robert Johnson[12] writes that such a divine, absolute merging with another partner has a limit in this world because

---

[12] Robert A. Johnson gave Carl Jung's complex theories a simplicity and elegance. His term 'inner work' has been adopted by seekers of his essence and the meaning of life. A lecturer and Jungian analyst,

we live in a dual universe where everything is limited and nothing is infinite.

As for those married couples who have already lived for fourteen years, have reached the twenty-one-year cycle, and have not remained in a formal relationship...

The universe begins to bless these couples as they continue to cling to each other, to intimacy. The universe is not stingy with gifts for them, which relate to boundless intimacy, boundless togetherness, and possibilities. This kind has a special status in the world and in society. The kin field of the family acquires the blessing of the White Moon, an angelic seal symbolising inviolability to evil.

The descendants of those who purge for themselves and for the family all the karma of intersex relations will have a high path of realisation, a special blessing to receive an open channel of love between a man and a woman. Already somewhere in the 17th or 18th year of their life together, they begin to have radically new opportunities: both financially and organisationally.

The universe shows that they are on the right track. But unfortunately, this is the period when people tend to get divorced.

However, if that doesn't happen, they as a couple become stronger than all the problems. They are tried and driven out of the world, they are under terrible pressure, they are

---

Johnson is the author of *He, She, We, Inner Work, Ecstasy, Transformation, and Dreams and Fantasies. Analysis and Use.*
In 1998, he published *Balancing Between Heaven and Earth*, a book of events, feelings and spiritual experiences from his own biography.

deprived of almost everything they have gained. So what do they do? They get married and thank the Lord; they finally have time to thank God for having each other.

My experience is that there is a direct correlation between a person's shortcomings and the karma they encounter in life. This karma is a chance to sort out what your set is that you were born with, your characteristics of soul, spirit, personality, ego. How this whole construct inside of you functions.

Karma trains you, due to the presence of another person, a form of exchange with the world of certain resources, which will in any case be difficult for you. And you will try to work out this scenario one way or another.

The practice of layouts is very widespread now, but there you enter into another's kin programs, you are a dead grandfather, a dead soldier, a dead woman. You cling all these stories to yourself, and your fate matrix closes, because by taking part in an unqualified shamanistic ritual, you impose a lot of alien matrixes on yourself.

In France, there is a very respected and recognised spiritual school, which uses a completely different methodology—ecological, invented at the dawn of civilisation, handed down to us by the keepers of this tradition.

It happens so that two people form a couple where one is a guardian angel for the other, but neither he nor she is aware of it.

I have seen such couples and if their personal karmic burdens were not too big, they could hold on in that relationship. Here, for example, is the union of Celine Dion and her now-deceased spouse. Celine is the richest singer in the world, but no one saw her naked or wearing pink feathers, running around the stage and making sexually scandalous provocations.

She has reached great heights in creativity, thanks not only to her talent but also to her husband's efforts. At the same time, their personal karma made her a widow.

There are no 'insignificant' people in our lives; everyone we have a certain type of relationship with.

There are many carriers of your karma on Earth. In order to make sure you receive this karma, fate begins to show them to you when it is time to work out the karmic aspects.

How to understand the difference between karmic predestination and the inability to defend your interests, traditions, self and so on? This question has plagued me for a long time. Is it necessary to build up these or those qualities and take control of the situation, or to heal it?

I made a lot of mistakes: when it was necessary to heal, I dealt with the situation, and then some time would pass, and I would get the same situation, suddenly multiplied tenfold, and from where I had not expected it at all.

I thought that I needed to fill my nature with qualitative characteristics, to go through this, to process myself, in order to finally close the situation. But when the same thing came to me, multiplied many times over, I realised that it was karma. However, it was already too late, and the second situation would come over my head.

Correspondingly, when, on the contrary, I had to make tough decisions, I thought it was karma, and I continued to heal it all. But trying to fix everything resulted in the fact that everything simply began to fall apart because the resources weren't going where they were supposed to, and the universe was showing that.

I spent a lot of time in these corridors, and then I developed a method of analysis that demonstrates what is really going on. It is not universal, and it may not work for everyone. But for me personally, where it is necessary to use some kind of violence against myself or others, against circumstances, to limit my free will, to impose something— this is already a karmic story.

If I can regulate the situation with discipline, negotiations, tools, light and ecological pressure, then the situation is in the zone of development of personal qualities. If I want to resolve the situation very much, if it makes me restless, if it twists me inside out, this is also a karmic sign.

And if I have a clear head and I see that I simply have to work very hard, but I don't feel like it...then it's more of an evolutionary process; you have to organise yourself somehow, and willy-nilly you start doing that. And usually I don't get twisted, but there's an awareness that I don't want to pull myself into this wagon, but I will pull myself into it and I will resolve the situation in a certain way. I use the same indicators when I analyse my relations with my inner circle.

If there is such a barrier that can only be overcome through violence, then it is definitely karma as fate, and the situation needs to be healed.

An interesting lesson for me in my time was that sometimes healing a situation solves it a billion times faster and more effectively if the right keys are chosen.

For example, a very difficult situation a woman has with her spouse is related to the fact that she is unhappy with everything, and any attempts to negotiate end in nothing. And only when she uses psycho-emotional manipulation, violence, blackmail, threats, then the situation is resolved. And she leaves the situation alone and begins to heal the situation with her mother-in-law.

All of her steps with regard to the family, her husband, her mother-in-law, the alignment of certain processes cause her to have a completely different attitude towards his family. While she leaves the man alone, suddenly her relationship with him changes dramatically.

All of these keys are picked up in a private session, when the analysis is carried out and the person chooses the tools for himself. But it is very important to understand that the skills needed here are complex. You also need to read books and attend training sessions. Energy and Psychology. Theoria cum praxis.[13]

If you are not set on studying yourself in depth, but on understanding quickly and without effort what you should do, this is also your culture of dialogue with yourself. But if you want to study yourself very deeply, and it's very important for you to build an ecological relationship with yourself, then spontaneous insights won't interest you at all. Because you are the Cosmos, and it is simply inappropriate to define yourself by one facet.

All your life is divided into periods and strictly regulated. In its first half, the most important thing for you is relations, children, family and kin, and in the second half nothing will be more important than the path to God.

You have two people, two destinies living inside of you, and because of that you are very difficult to communicate,

---

13 Theory with Practice (lat.)

because you are dual. There is always another nature residing in you, which wants another, and also life is rigidly divided into periods. It is such a special fate when you experience cardinally polar values during one life.

And you subconsciously feel that, and you can't, definitively, either settle down with the family or go into spirituality, and career and business...that's a problem area for you, too. It's something that you have to come to terms with and find a comfortable option of realisation.

الصَّبُورُ

Part III
The Alchemy of Intimacy

What Is Intimacy?

Today, it is the most valuable product of the intangible. Our lives, our social structures, the psychological patterns of society, and the economy are evolving in such a way that intangible values are becoming increasingly important and expensive.

There is a transition from a production society to an information society, and all sorts of IT, consulting and communication products are worth many times more than tangible assets, which are rapidly becoming obsolete. Intangible assets of a psychological nature are growing in value, which corresponds to the general paradigm of society's development.

The quality of intimacy is an incredibly valuable and scarce asset in society. Through your knowledge of intimacy, you receive tremendous advantages in building your social strategy, your career, and your life path.

Imagine some very high-quality service, a social institution in which everyone is in a state of mutual alienation. Such an institution is commercially unprofitable. People would call it a bad service. None of them will link it directly to a lack of intimacy. But they will not feel that the staff, the head, the managers are interested in a close relationship with the customer. That they are close to them, and therefore, dear and important.

Today's relationship professionals are struggling to teach employees the art of intimacy in business. So that those can build relationships with business partners in which they feel that their interests are your interests, and you act out of intimacy, not alienation or coldness.

And the competition of some goods or, for example, the competition through appearances in intersex or partnership relationships are forms of competition that will become obsolete. Today, in fact, any woman is able to do anything she wants with her appearance, if she has such a task. She can reshape her face, completely change her external image.

So many women are actively doing this, but in the end, in the space of love (if you can use the word 'victory' here), the winner is not the one who coped with their appearance, but the one who knows what intimacy is, and can give it. And this will be her victory for herself, her maximum satisfaction and the opportunity to choose the right qualities of her partner.

Intimacy is security, it is relaxation, it is a state in which you find direct contact with the heart, with the soul of the person with whom you are communicating.

Today, the pace of life is accelerating. We travel, we change real estate, social space, tastes and preferences. Even if we are limited in space, living in a village or a small village, the Internet allows us to plan and redesign our lives very actively. In this accelerated pace, intimacy begins to take on a special value; we miss it very much; we don't have enough time for it; we don't quite understand the laws by which it develops; we feel that we lack intimacy with ourselves.

Without building a relationship of intimacy in business, you're going to spend too much energy to mitigate the risks. And I think that such a relationship will be very difficult to capitalise. You will be busy all the time guarding your boundaries in contracts, in documents, in paperwork, and in negotiations.

You will spend up to 70 per cent of your resources on this; it is sometimes very difficult to make a net profit in such a situation because a lot of resources are diverted by keeping your boundaries in check.

So, intimacy is a very marketable commodity. Techniques such as networking or negotiations with VIPs are now spreading very actively. But these techniques don't solve the problem, because if you use them in a state of stiffness and don't know which traumas of intimacy you have and which your partner has, then you stay at the level of social manipulation.

We see people who want to connect with us just fine. But those who have resources try to close themselves off from such connections, to fence themselves off because they very clearly distinguish the hunt for resources from the technologies of intimacy. A person with a sense of intimacy within themselves, appearing in space, instantly receives all acquaintances and resources; all doors are open to them.

See the difference? Either to get sophisticated in social manipulation and then guard your boundaries in contracts. Or be so close to people, like them so much, that they will seek your company and try to create a relationship with you in the language of intimacy that you broadcast, that you create with your business partners.

Let's look at what people usually confuse intimacy with. To do this, let's work with definitions.

Intimacy is not acceptance and recognition of you. We very often confuse it with some other emotional, psychological need that has an expiration date. So how is intimacy different from them?

The need to be beautiful, to be admired and fall in love with you, to give you attention and gifts; the need to have children; the need to build something; the need to earn money; the need to create; the need to create and express yourself. They all have their cyclical stages, and these needs are not always relevant.

But, for example, the need for intimacy is a basic need, without which the psyche, emotionality begins to suffer, to experience crises. There are studies proving that after two weeks of lack of qualitative intimacy in your life, you begin to experience psychological frustration and emotional disorders. That is, emotional health is disturbed by any instability, anxiety, depressed mood, repetitive intrusive thoughts, internal crisis of feelings, dissatisfaction.

Why does all this happen? The reason is in the lack of intimacy energy, when you do not know where and how to take it, how to deal with it correctly, or when you have a trauma of this intimacy.

Your psyche, oddly enough, will remain healthy if, for example, you don't have a sexual partner at all in your life. If you don't get, say, the recognition or respect in society that matches your emotional ambitions. Surprisingly, contrary to your beliefs, you will feel good about yourself even if you don't meet someone who will love you as yourself and serve you in that love.

But! Your emotional health will be ruined if you don't have regular, constant sources of multidimensional intimacy in your life.

The psyche is set up in such a way that you need to take this as a postulate, and take it really seriously. When you feel an acute crisis of intimacy, you begin to fill it at the expense of the attention of others: a beauty specialist, a massage therapist, a concierge, a salesman in the store. You try to compensate for the lack of intimacy in all kinds of surrogate ways, as psyche pushes for this.

You unconsciously seek out sources of intimacy, you cannot afford not to provide them. If you one day stop doing this, your emotional health will be in a very precarious state.

Intimacy is needed from birth to death in its entirety and all the time, and is precisely why it is a special phenomenon.

It's one thing to interact with resources and emotional needs that are limited in time, such as before age 40, 50, 70. Or to experience a relationship crisis when meeting, breaking up, forming a family, having children: all these things come and go.

The state of intimacy, which is basic from birth to death, is quite another matter, as necessary as air. It dictates different rules, laws and, therefore, completely different approaches to understanding and creating such an important resource. Its insufficiency or imperfection causes special, specific crises.

So: what should not be confused with intimacy?

Intimacy shouldn't be confused with acceptance. People may not be intimate with you, but they have accepted and acknowledged you.

Intimacy is not love. Love is a very special state. You may be loved very much, but you may not be given intimacy. Some of the women know this story very well.

"I feel that this man loves me, I feel our passion, I feel our empathy, we can have amazing sexual intimacy, we are united in values and interests, but I cannot relax with this man. We have conflicts because of misunderstandings and because of some feeling of mismatch, as if we don't live with the same pace…I can't even explain what it is."

That is, love can come into your life without intimacy. And without love, oddly enough, you can survive, because love is a global universal energy, you can receive it not only from another person, but from God, from some other sources. But if love has come into your life without the energy of intimacy, you have to build up this intimacy; love will not guarantee you this intimacy.

Intimacy is not trust. People can trust you very much in something, but still not be intimate to you.

Friendship is not intimacy.

Respect, recognition of your right, your name, your position in public space gives you a certain status in the system of relations and in the collective, but it is not intimacy, nor is inclusion in some kind of community.

I would very much like you not to confuse intimacy and these categories. If you need any of these states, and your life lacks these energies, you should compensate them.

However, it happens very often that the person who needs intimacy is not able to realise it. Having some kind of trauma, not having been taught the culture of intimacy, the person, wanting it, tries to achieve everything that was listed above. But these are all intangible values of life. Yes, they are of course very important, but we earn them, we get them, we have to justify them. We create them, we are the creators and builders of this intangible energy resource.

Of course, we need recognition and acceptance, love and friendship, status and position in society. All this contributes to psychological health, but it is not intimacy. And very often a person, desiring intimacy, gets it all. In a good sense, they psychologically serve the space, they are very attentive to people, form harmonious relationships with them, creates these values around themselves.

But in the end, they are left devastated as they close the door behind them, finds themselves alone with themselves, and realise that something is missing where the heart is. And a subtle sadness, a subtle sense of longing, a feeling of missing something visit them.

And in that moment, they say, "Lord, I love You. What is wrong with me? Why, having all these blessings, having given sweat and blood for them, having created a family, business relationships, acquired friends, do I, nevertheless, feel more than just loneliness? Why do I, a mature person, feel a kind of isolation and an inability to fully share my space of life with those around me?."

So, intimacy is neither love, nor friendship, nor acceptance—these are completely separate states, separate categories. But what is the quality of intimacy that fills the soul, that is intimately connected with our immortal self, that gives absolute spiritual stability in life? This energy is closest to the feeling of God in another person.

I will give you a few allegories so that your psyche will form an associative field and you will be able to experience this subtle sensation.

It is a harmony permeating your whole being, an intuitive vision of the essence of things, a special affinity with the way the world or the other person is arranged. Intimacy is a state where someone intuitively reads you without words, sensing who you are in essence, and without making gross mistakes about you.

They unconsciously, very subtly, pick up such gifts, commit such actions, say such words, appear there and then that you clearly understand: this person feels you from within, experiences the same as you, thanks to a special inner contact with you. And, when you experience such a relationship, you suddenly realise that for you it is an affair with your soul, with your spirit.

You are lifted up and swirled by the energy of an incredible magnetic relationship in which your interlocutor is part of yourself.

Through the energy of intimacy, God has made us happy to be united with the mystery of His creation, with the higher intuition, with the hidden meaning of events. He has given us the ability to be in a marvellous ecstatic dance with the universe, experiencing an incomparable intimacy with the world or with a person as a supreme revelation. You begin to see and feel that you are part of Creation.

Everything is in its place. God conceived everything incomparably harmoniously, and you feel that intimacy is also a very deep attention on some deep level of spirit and soul, which is undividedly given only to you and settles beside you, warming your heart and soul.

For example, you come to a negotiation tired from standing in traffic. You are ready for the standard process of negotiations according to the rules of the meeting, protocol and the hierarchy of business priorities. You take the elevator, dressed according to a strict dress code. You are in an atmosphere of intense anticipation, of stress.

But in the negotiation room in front of you, there is a man who looks deep inside you and understands you without words. And negotiations with him are not in the usual, formal scenario. It is not even a negotiation, it is a desire to move together in the same direction, reading each other like an open book, to be in a state of intuitive harmony, without violating personal boundaries. It is something like a synchronised harmonious dance.

This is the kind of gift of intimacy God can give without giving love. Maybe that person will tell you, "I don't quite recognise the value of your business competencies." But when there is intimacy, you, hearing such an assessment, are ready to grow higher than the mountains and fly higher than the birds because you become terribly curious about what is meant.

For some reason, it doesn't traumatise you; you're not fixated on the fact that you're losing and may not get the reward that's due. You're interested in something else entirely—what this person thinks, says, and feels, what they're going through. For you, their worldview is incredibly valuable and interesting.

And when they see it, they become indifferent to the business side of your dialogue with them, because there is nothing higher and more valuable than the free flow of energy. Energy and consciousness, very closely interrelated, are above material values, for they are responsible for who and among whom you will be tomorrow.

The accumulation of the quality of intimacy in the soul leads to the fact that the gaze of some people penetrates into the hearts of others, and between them the invisible bridges are built through which love, sex, power, friendship, money, and creative fulfilment move freely. You get both growth, assistance and recommendations, and new and increasingly unique offers and invitations that so many professionals, perhaps working better than you, have no idea about.

You, speaking to the world in the language of intimacy, have caravans of life's benefits, relationships, wonderful people, incredible creative events, trips, travels moving across these bridges. It's as if you're being swept along by the flow.

Let us summarise some of the results. The first essential competence is the differentiation of emotional states: what is intimacy and what is not.

Intimacy is a basic psychological resource. If you want to stay emotionally healthy, minimise stress and tension, and remove struggle from your life; you must consider emotional states, relationships, and the competencies of intimacy as basic, priorities. And, just from intimacy, you can create love, gain acceptance and friendships, be included in the community and benefit from sound advice, build a family, a partnership, a business together.

Based on intimacy, all of this will be on an entirely different, immeasurably higher level.

Since intimacy is very closely connected with the feeling of flow, of wonder, of opening up the field of life around you, it is obvious that it is also connected to your soul. The ability to be in intimacy is a special interaction of the soul with psyche, emotionality, and communicative competence. Your soul, being in harmony, at peace, in a state of acceptance, and connecting with your consciousness, draws on your psychology and helps you to discover your life potential.

This is the gift God has placed in each of us by creating an outlet for this channel of intimacy.

Let's take a look at what is called a KPI system—key performance indicators in business. How do we know that we have entered the space of intimacy, that it has emerged and is engaged?

The criteria for working intimacy energy are as follows.

The first is safety. If intimacy is present as an emotional competence, a quality of your condition, an earned circle of relationship, then you will feel that your life is safe. Intimacy greatly and significantly reduces the anxiety factor. Imagine that a woman needs to get married, she wants to have a baby, being at that marginal fertile age, when it is an actual biological, generic, spiritual task for her. Nothing about her, let's say, argues with that task.

But, it's one thing when she has 8 suitors, and they're all right for her, and she just has to decide who her heart is closer to. It's another thing when she doesn't know how to build relationships with men out of intimacy. These two cases are radically different in their levels of anxiety and sense of security.

If you have the energy of intimacy in your life, you feel that you are safe. You are protected by the people with whom you are close, as well as the knowledge and information flows due to intimacy with the right people.

The next criterion for the effectiveness of being in intimacy and having that energy in your life is naturalness. You feel that you do not need to strain too much to earn

157

money, to build a family, to achieve something, to become a professional. Everything comes naturally to you.

Those who are close to you, knowing your interests, will help with recommendations, advice, acquaintances, and if you lack some contacts, you will easily enter a space of intimacy with those who can share the necessary resources with you.

You'll feel that you're conserving energy rather than being exhausted like a squirrel in a wheel, because you're not anxious, because everything goes naturally because you're in intimacy with those hearts and those people for whom you are part of their world, of their worldview.

It's also very important that intimacy makes you feel positively relaxed. If you have a business intimacy with your boss, and he calls you to a meeting, you think you need to grab a box of chocolates bought especially for him in Belgium and regale him with a story about your vacation. You ponder, based on the category of intimacy about how pleasant it will be for you to interact.

You're not stressed, you're not producing adrenaline, you're not overwhelmed with negative emotions. On the contrary, you are proceeding from the fact that it will be pleasant for you to interact on any topic now.

I will share a very interesting observation. Among my clients there is a young man who is not yet 18, and with whom we started practising quite early. His particular genotype and strong psychological health allowed him to take very serious adult sessions when he was still a teenager. We were going through intimacy topics, in particular the technique of building close relationships with teachers at school.

It was time to plan for the future, it was time for exams, summing up, solving certain problems together with teachers and students. No one called this boy's parents to school, since all the teachers preferred to do without their involvement. The parents were told, "We have such contact with your child that we, in general, do not even consider it necessary to bother you, because we interact directly."

Seeing this attitude of the teachers towards this boy, who was already a legend at school, his classmates could not understand why he had such influence; why he was taken into account; why his opinion was so important? This, of course, created public intrigue about what was going on. Is he a toady? Or maybe he's bribing? Or somehow manipulates those around him? Why do people like this get preferential treatment, why are they, as they say, the darlings of the world?

The secret lies, of course, in the quality of intimacy within the person himself and in the fact that he understands that this is a basic resource, and, at the same time, a scarce one. Everyone searches hard for it but no one can grasp and realise the magic of the language of intimacy with oneself and with the world.

We will view intimacy as a spiritual, energetic practice. As a personal style of being, as the art of creating reality and life itself, and interacting with it from a point of intimacy. We will view intimacy as that space that we begin to create with special competence. As a way of ecologically exchanging emotional and material resources with the world.

To awaken imaginative thinking, I suggest we look at intimacy as the energy of water, the basis of life, binding all the elements in the world and carrying information. The entire field energy-information structure is written in the structure of water. Water is the planetary memory, the planetary psychic body.

Dipping your hands into a natural body of water, you will feel how water literally embraces you, how it instantly becomes close to you. It represents the quality of intimacy. Warm water warms you, cold water cools you, a cold rain invigorates you. In the same way, the climate of your inner intimacy energetically affects those around you immediately.

Maybe there are water lilies blooming in your inner reservoir, and you are a quiet and level person. Maybe you feel like a narrow little river that's drying up, or an empty lake that's shallowing. Or maybe, on the contrary, there's a stage in your life right now when you feel like an ocean and are taking over more and more land. This background state is a metaphor for your inner body of water—the first small practical exercise.

The energy of intimacy binds all the fabric of life, it permeates everywhere, is the foundation of everything, being a kind of dampening medium for all the other senses. When these feelings flow from us, we exchange them, easily attract love, easily enter into friendships, harmoniously solve difficult, crisis issues.

A lot of psychological resources in life are built up, and intimacy is an integral part of being, and we don't have to do anything to create it. Intimacy is an instant alchemical reaction, which in milliseconds, leaping between people, removes any burdens, worries and cares. It allows you to trust your resources without building rigid boundaries because it gives birth to a sense of security.

It's a quality of being, on which not time is spent, but energy of the mind, heart and soul. And if someone tells you that in order to build intimacy with a certain person you need to invest time, then they don't want to build intimacy with you, they are trying to get some completely different resource from you.

In fact, when we are rich, beautiful, young, abundant, very often, unfortunately, people are not drawn to us out of intimacy. And then we all the more need to understand: intimacy is about what? And, why are all kinds of resource relationships different from what intimacy is about?

Intimacy is a state of being, and if the other person is not ready to share it, there are two possible outcomes. Either the energy of intimacy is not awakened in this person, and you will become its messenger for him. Or this person is initially near you not out of intimacy, but because of a different motivational, exchange, resource process, and this is a completely different message for the relationship on a completely different level.

This is why it is very important when there seems to be insufficient time for intimacy, not to waste time on something that only appears to be intimacy.

Again, intimacy is a quality of being, it is not a doing. And, if people want intimacy, they may not see each other for years, but every time when they are in touch, they feel that this very golden bridge has been laid between them, over which there is a free and very generous exchange of experiences, life values, relationships, connections from one shore of abundance to the other.

Intimacy with Ourselves

How do you make sustained intimacy with yourself? What is, in general, the criterion for intimacy with oneself? Let's get into it now. Let's go back to the exercise "intimacy with oneself, qualities of intimacy with oneself" and look at this topic from a practical perspective.

The first item you note is called "My abandoned, unloved parts." Answer the questions: "What parts of myself do I dislike? Why have I abandoned them or do I want to abandon them? What is my distance to those parts?"

For example, I don't like that part of my psyche, my life, in myself that gets sick from time to time. Everyone has that part that causes them to experience some really painful condition. And when it becomes the main part of your life and you become a person in pain, it is difficult for you to alienate that part from yourself. You want it to leave you alone, you don't consider that you have a 'we' in common with it, and you say, "God, I wish it would leave my life and my space."

Make a list now of the parts that you reject, that you can't give love to for various reasons. Try to find the abandoned parts of the psyche. These are the ridicule, the resentment, the vilification that caused you stress long ago, as a child.

You need to write down for yourself the needs of these parts that you haven't met in time, that have made them deficient for you. These are the parts that will fight within you against intimacy with yourself, that rebel and prevent you from accepting yourself wholly as you are. You need to understand what needs are behind those parts, what you have not given yourself in life, find ways to heal those needs, appease those parts and then give those parts love within yourself.

This is what is called the work of healing intimacy with your life, with yourself. This is how you will come to a state where all you need is your one existence, your one life, to feel incredible intimacy with yourself. The fact that you are awake, that you have a body, that you are living, breathing, you exist—that will be enough for you. This will give you a completely different energetic state with a feeling of an enormous reserve of energy, inner strength, and mental comfort.

The state of intimacy with yourself heals from co-dependency. After all, the deficit parts that you're describing right now are pushing you into a co-dependent relationship with other people and with yourself.

There's no peace—there's this propeller constantly spinning around inside that's tearing you apart, and you're experiencing internal conflicts and contradictions. At this point, of course, you are not in intimacy with yourself, you are in co-dependence with these parts; they manipulate you because they have unmet needs. When you learn to meet these needs properly, when you heal the deficits, you begin to love these parts, even if they remain the same.

For example, the indulger mother will still remain inside you, but if you know how to heal her, fill her, soothe her, you will have a completely different attitude towards her. You will love her in yourself, because you will realise that she makes you a good mother learning from her mistakes.

You will begin to cooperate with those parts inside, and the dialogue from intimacy with yourself will become a growth of intimacy space from the inside out. You will begin to create a relationship around yourself in which you will be, above all, intimacy-oriented with your partner.

I have commented on the quality of intimacy with yourself and shown how it breaks down, what makes it happen, how you come to it. Of course, I wish you quality intimacy with yourselves at the level of harmonious acceptance of yourself, your life, and the understanding that you are free from any point, from any being, no matter how your affairs go, no matter how you feel right now, to move into a state of harmony and a quality state of intimacy.

The Difference Between Intimacy and Love

Let's talk about the difference between intimacy and love.

But, let me tell you, isn't love between a man and a woman manifested just on the level of intimacy? If not, it's not love, but some other form of relationship.

Unfortunately or fortunately, while love and intimacy—these sisters of evolutionary experience—are very closely related, indeed love can exist without intimacy. Think of Rhett Buttler and Scarlett O'Hara's relationship in *Gone with the Wind*. You can't doubt that he loved her, but would he have succeeded in building a relationship of intimacy? No.

What is love? It is the cumulative vibration of God. It is all seven rays of Him, all seven shades, seven notes, seven manifestations, seven qualities, when they all add up to one whole. This state of absolute wholeness is the perfect body of God.

This love may lack, for example, a ray of intimacy, a ray of faithfulness, or a ray of service. But in the aggregate, a person is already initiated in the body of God's love, and their soul—especially if the parents loved each other at the moment of conception—comes through this channel of love. While the parents may lack certain qualities for love to become the full cycle of divine consciousness, the full cycle of all the light vibrations on the planet.

Intimacy is one of the lightest, most important vibrations of the love channel. And so you can experience love, although its circle is not yet filled mentally and energetically, the closure of the love space has not yet happened, when love becomes unconditional, divine. After all, we know that there is love between parents and children, between a man and a woman, and there is universal, all-absorbing, all-encompassing, unconditional, cosmic love.

It's an entirely different quality, which maybe you've never even met in your lifetime. To switch to such a vibration of love, you have to have another level of spiritual movement, of the fullness of spiritual life. And sometimes it happens that you have gathered from the whole channel of love only one-third of all the qualities, but it is already enough for love to appear in your life.

The rays of service, acceptance, and absence of selfishness may be revealed in it, but, for example, intimacy, self-denial, self-sacrifice are not included yet, and your love has not yet become divine and holy. Love is all the rays of God gathered in one channel when the fullness of these qualities in anahata is revealed.

And intimacy is that vibration within love that helps you connect soul and spirit, consciousness and soul movement. It is responsible for connecting with the world, with God's plan, with other people. This is the kind of vibration that is the conductor, the very water that helps to connect all states, feelings and energies.

And if your love is without intimacy, then you need to build up this quality in your love treasury. If you are reading

166

this book now, it means that your current evolutionary stage of development is working out the vibration of intimacy on the divine level for your anahata.

For the idly curious, the Lord will not spill out information on how to build intimacy from such a source. You are reading these lines—it means that this is your stage of evolution. You have already developed a very large spectrum of qualities within the channel of love.

It's time to absorb the vibration of intimacy on the universal, divine level, when you are connected by a golden thread with the whole world, with God, and through intimacy you feel other people and your own life path.

If you are in intimacy with God and with your soul, through this you know what your path is, where you are going, and what you need right now. Opening the channel of intimacy gives superpowers of clairvoyance because if you are close to people, God and yourself, your resources are limitless.

People with unmet needs and deficits mythologise and idolise intimacy and envy those who have it. In their mind, it is a free trough: "Since we are close to the great, rich, beautiful and strong, it means we will travel in golden carriages and live in luxury villas." They do not understand the underlying inner mechanism that drives this process, and so they are left with nothing.

Intimacy Between Man and Woman as Partners

It is the intimacy of women with their male parts, and for men with their female parts. Whether or not we have qualitative intimacy with our sexual partner greatly affects our creativity and inspiration and how open we are to this world in terms of our overall appeal in life.

To figure out what qualitative intimacy with a man is, let's look at what its counterweight is. On one side of the scale is intimacy with a man, and on the other side is not loneliness, as you might think, not separation, not resentment, not loss, but the freedom of your partner.

These scales must be in balance at all times. Experiencing certain deficits, we tend to overload the intimacy bowl when we are in a relationship. We idealise intimacy with our sexual partner, and it becomes something vital to us. We increase the importance of this factor in our lives because our health is tied to it: with qualitative intimacy, we feel completely different on the level of our body, psyche and emotions.

But what is freedom? How to properly differentiate it and give it to the partner, how not to choke him with your intimacy? What mistakes women and men often make?

Women are emotional creatures, and our mistakes are more noticeable because we scatter them around, multiplied by the power of our own emotional experiences.

The partner's freedom in intimacy consists of the following states: freedom of movement, freedom of information, freedom to build relationships in the society and in the world the way he wants.

Freedom of movement. Anyone has the right to move their body and their consciousness as they see fit: to go where they see fit, to stay there for a while. And to choose those places for themselves.

Freedom of information means that any person has the right to take an interest in what is important to them, drawing from those sources that are relevant to them, to exchange this information, to express their opinion and to defend their position in life.

Finally, there is also the freedom to have in life those relationships, those connections, those communications that this person needs for their development.

Without these three freedoms, our psyche cannot function normally, since we do not become ourselves, cannot be human beings in the full sense of the word. Very often, when we enter into a relationship of intimacy, we begin to claim these freedoms in the life of the partner. This destroys intimacy because when our freedom is in balance, so is our intimacy, and both are in harmony within our heart and soul.

It is very important to understand that your partner's freedom is not an area of your trauma. When they enjoy freedom in these three aspects, they are exercising a person's natural right to live their life the way they want to. This is an incredibly important point. It shouldn't hurt you because of your neglected, unmet needs, any trauma or deficits.

Very often when we experience a lack of intimacy, when we get into a relationship, the first thing we do is begin to sweep our partner's freedom into the territory of intimacy. But intimacy grows in parallel with the quality of our partner's freedom, because these two categories, these two realities exist simultaneously.

For instance, the man declares: "We'll go on vacation together but we'll stay in separate rooms and meet three times a week for lunch. The rest of the time I have to work, and we won't see each other." He has already given her no freedom of movement and no freedom to choose her relationship, including with him. This means that intimacy between them has entered a state of crisis, and its level, its quality has begun to fall rapidly.

The art of intimacy with your sexual partner lies in the fact that you help them to build up their level of freedom, and, at the same time, keep your own at a qualitative level. You have a culture of forming this space of freedom, you have elevated it to the rank of a psychological art. You actively use these freedoms yourself, you grant them to yourself.

A person who has the freedom of movement, exchange of information and building relationships with other people has an inexhaustible resource for building quality relationships based on intimacy. But very often, because we have trauma of need, trauma of intimacy, and a partner begins to take advantage of these freedoms, we decide that all of this threatens our intimacy.

We try hard to take away the territory of freedom in order to expand the boundaries of our intimacy. But this is a fundamentally wrong strategy; it leads to a situation in which there is neither freedom nor intimacy. These two phenomena—like two sisters, like the Earth and the Moon—always walk together, coexist in our psyche simultaneously and in parallel.

You help your partner to develop their quality of freedom, to discover its new criteria, to share your own experience with your partner. You help them to expand their horizons of life, and when they see that you support their freedom, they begin to build up the quality of intimacy with you. This is a very important point, because intimacy is something that is both inside and outside, and something that is impossible if the three forms of freedom are not present.

No relationship is worth your sacrificing these three forms. There are no kinds of relationships that are ecological if the three forms of freedom in life do not exist. Note that there is no cheating here. We are not talking about the freedom to change sexual partners. Freedom of relationship is the freedom to be interested in the people with whom one wants to get to know, with whom one wants to establish emotional intimacy.

You may say: well, today they have met, tomorrow they like each other, then they have developed emotional closeness, and in the end, they have decided to live together. This is the very concept that points to a very deep trauma of intimacy within you and means that you basically do not have a balance of freedom and intimacy within you.

You have a very painful model formed in which you are initially programming the scenario exactly in this way, with the kind of fears that I just described.

It's bad if we don't have these freedoms for ourselves, don't know how to use them. If we don't have them formed as criteria of quality and value of life, of respect for ourselves, of providing ourselves with quality resources. Because in this case, we are jealous of our partner's freedom, and of course, this is the position of a victim. And sacrifice is already a deficit and therefore, manipulation and loss of energy of qualitative intimacy.

The mature, healthy part grown inside of you, with room to move and inform, its own circle of relationships and all the freedoms, will protect you emotionally, provide the opportunity to expand your boundaries. And, the wider your life boundaries, the more resources, the stronger the energy, and therefore, the more filling your intimacy with unique experiences and quality of energy, life, information.

Such a saturated person, living in an aura of freedom, in a state of openness to the world, is impossible to tear away from because this kind of intimacy is bottomless. From this energy of freedom, we draw the energy of paired intimacy, the energy of fidelity.

There is an important point that needs to be understood very clearly. The fact is that if your partner has not only been in physical sexual contact with another person but has been with them in heart, mind, soul, created a common 'we' on all levels—physical, emotional, spiritual—this is called adultery. When a person commits real adultery, you need to understand very clearly that after this common 'we' relationship on the level of intimacy in the couple is no longer there.

There is no way to glue it back together. It kills the relationship. They simply end, and it is unreal to build them anew.

Once you realise this, you will realise that there is no in-between form between a real 'we' in intimacy and only the decision to change. If a person decides to go out of their way to change and kill your relationship, then restricting their freedoms will not help the situation. You will simply become a victim and a manipulator. Cheating kills the relationship, and that means you will lose it and your partner anyway; it will be gone from your life.

If you are in intimacy with yourself, you have a lot of mental resources because you love and accept all parts of yourself; you have a lot of freedom, a wide range of acquaintances and communication. In this case, you will not perceive your partner's desire to change and destroy your life together as a colossal trauma, after which you will never get back on your feet. You will understand the fatality, the inevitability of what is to come.

You will surrender freedoms, help the other to build up these freedoms, give these freedoms to yourself, bless your partner to have all these forms of freedom. At the same time, you will clearly understand that if he or she uses these freedoms to kill your relationship, there is nothing you can do here. If he or she is set, programmed to kill your relationship, he or she will do it no matter what.

If he or she will kill it all, then it was unsustainable. We are not talking about fate now, but about the ecology of the intimacy space in a sexual relationship, and what it is made of.

It's very important to understand that freedom gives a person qualitative emotional security. But if you have fear in your heart and deny your partner the freedom to perceive the world as they want, to get to know you, to exchange information, to meet alone, to be intimate with those with whom they want, then do not expect to have qualitative intimacy, because intimacy is a disinterested exchange.

"I am open to you in the void, and you are open to me in the void, and we don't need anything from each other." If you have to realise some of your fears and eliminate emotional deficits in the relationship, then you lose emotional security. Without freedom, there is no emotional security or qualitative intimacy.

Do you think you give yourself the freedom to move around, the freedom to inform, the freedom to build a relationship? How willing are you to support your partner in these freedoms? If not, what fears do you have and what challenges do you face in this context?

The source of trauma that prevents you from combining intimacy and freedom has its origins in adolescence, and for the normal development of modern person it is the absolute norm. Yet all of these complexities can be recognised, healed, and put in their proper place.

An adolescent who ceases to be a child often finds themselves in a situation in which they seek both love and freedom, and unsuccessfully. Above all, they seek it from their parents, and parents often fail to properly initiate the teen into this freedom, to properly give it. Perhaps some people remember the state of wanting so badly to put on nice sneakers, jeans, grab a tape recorder and meet up with friends.

And some may have smoked, some may have participated in some other experiments of mastering the territory of freedom. But always, unfortunately, we didn't get it where the family was, and we didn't get it where love was. We were winning it back in the outside world.

And inside of us at that moment, a model of how you can give yourself all the freedom to be accepted by your parents in all the aspects in which a teenager experiments: movement, information, relationships, was not formed.

You don't give these freedoms to your partner or to yourself not because you have any sexual, sensual traumas. Not because you have some kind of negative relationship experience specifically in sex with your partners. Not because you have some kind of fatal destiny and you personally can't build the relationship of your dreams.

The root is hidden in your transition, your adolescence, when you didn't initiate in time and didn't pass that milestone, that experience of freedom being compatible with love. You didn't have someone by your side who fully encouraged all forms of your freedoms directly in your home, in your apartment. Your parents may have encouraged, say, one kind, for example, freedom of information, because you read everything, learn everything, perceive everything, but they may have restricted all other kinds.

And an adolescent from puberty for three years has this period in which they have to work up this pattern of balancing intimacy and emergent freedom. Because without freedom, there is no adult personality, but inner complexes, fears, victims. All these parts within us, all these unmet needs to combine love and freedom, intimacy and freedom, needs for their acceptance, support, approval—from adolescence.

Later, all this is transferred to the relationship with the partner, and we begin to experience very complicated emotions and states when they accept to use these freedoms. On top of that, we are not the people who can competently, ecologically help our partner to build up and expand them even more, and use them not as a tool to steal freedom.

Don't start seeing their boundaries of freedom as the territory of your own traumas. You will only be able to be like children with everyone around you and have intimacy when you have a tremendous amount of freedom of all three kinds behind you, provided with all the resources. You help your partner accumulate and use them to learn more about themselves and the world, to develop as a person, and to enrich your life through what they develop and enrich themselves.

Freedom cannot be abused. If a person is trying to do so, then they are traumatised, deficient. When a person uses the resource of movement, of information, of relationships, and treats some of their needs, some of their trauma, that is not freedom. They are not ready for freedom, they don't know what it is; they just can't have intimacy with you at all yet because they can't get out of a state in which they have deficits and needs in these three kinds of resources.

These three words do not mean freedom to them, but deficits. When a person uses resources to fill their deficits, of course it will destroy the relationship because they are busy covering their deficits, they cannot offer you qualitative intimacy; it is a completely different psychological state.

If you weren't taught as a teenager how to 'get off the coast', how to keep your relationship with your parents based on intimacy, and at the same time, start a sex life, implement everything you want, look the way you want, communicate with the people you want, go where you want, then you just haven't passed that experience. You are evolutionarily stuck on it and continue to be in relationships at the level of puberty.

We remain in relationships as teenagers trying to get past that milestone and learn both, male and female, how to combine intimacy and freedom in a relationship. It goes very hard and difficult and often drains the resource of the relationship. And after learning how to do this, they can simply break up because they may no longer be enough for further intimacy.

I suggest figuring out where the boundaries of your freedom are for you and how you give it to yourself. How you expand these boundaries, how you use them, how you project your fears of freedom onto your partner, trying to limit them, because for you this is love. When your parents tried to regulate your freedoms instead of teaching you how to use them and expand them endlessly, the following inference formed in your mind.

Love is a limitation of the other person's freedom; I care about them, no matter what happens, no matter how the family falls apart, and so within myself I look out for them.

If there is an energy of pure freedom inside, and one sincerely gives it to oneself and the other, then instantly such a qualitative intimacy is formed, which is stronger than anything else in the world. This basic psychic energy is necessary for you as the 'fuel' of your life, and is the foundation of your mental health.

And escape to freedom is escape to freedom, not freedom itself. Indeed, we ran away from our parents. No one taught us about freedom, we don't know how to expand and use it, and we experience a huge number of fears, very often shifting it all to our relationship with our partner, with whom we can't give ourselves or them freedom.

If, for example, freedom for yourself in information often supersedes the other two forms, it means that you are abusing something. If you are dependent on some concepts, on thought activity, it is certainly impossible to say that you are free in the field of information. Because freedom is universal, it means absolute access to all resources, which correspond to your level of development.

And it is expressed in the fact that you will choose that information, which is useful for you and contributes to the development of your individuality, life plans.

Once you have dealt with your adolescent traumas (freedom in intimacy, freedom in relationships, personal boundaries of freedom of the other person), you will instantly begin to accumulate qualitative intimacy, and you will inevitably come to the point where your common 'we' will acquire universality, you will become one Tao, one person.

I am sure that you will find a billion proofs of what I have just told you in yourselves. You will see how you have killed intimacy in relationships and perhaps continue to do so by not being able to be free yourself in those relationships and to give freedom to your partner. As a result, the quality of intimacy, the quality of energy in the relationship, drops.

Enforced Intimacy

Intimacy is the lot of those who actually do the work at work. They solve very many of life's problems at the expense of creative resources, and they build intimacy in purity, with people who are not self-interested. This does not mean that there cannot be a commodity-money relationship between them, or that they will not introduce each other to useful people.

Functionality will be present, but its importance will fade away against the deep satisfaction of contact with what the other person represents. This sincerity cannot be replaced by anything.

Sometimes a person, once in this or that space, fills it entirely with themselves, their meanings, their tasks, their tension. They come in and bring the energy of all their problems, which instantly cuts off the channel of intimacy between you and the world because you start fighting, having passed to the level of instincts, for survival.

Watch a movie that shows these psychological mechanisms very clearly. It's called *Coyote Ugly* and it's about a girl from the province trying to settle down in a big city. She has recorded her own songs on CDs and, wants to become a famous singer, goes around the recording studios and offers her demo record. In one scene, she is clearly explained what I am about to tell you.

She holds out the CDs to a woman, initiating her into the circumstances of her life, telling her that she comes from the province, wants to be a great singer, and no one takes her CDs. In a word, she begins to 'load' the woman down.

The woman sitting in front of her responds with absolutely golden, stunning words, presenting a lesson, a gift from a higher power. "Honey, you know, I was a single mother and raised my daughter alone. She became a lesbian, abandoned me, and now I live all alone, on a miserable salary. No one loves me and no one wants me."

The girl is taken aback and looks at her in utter bewilderment. "Well, darling, are you interested in this? Do you want it?"

The girl says, "No."

And the woman sums it up: "You know, Neither do I—all that stuff you're carrying around with you, I don't want it either."

This is where a culture of very high quality, deep psychohygiene emerges. If you have deficits in functional exchange, growth needs, compensation and balance, talk to specialists. Psychologists, therapists, even beauty salon staff will gladly listen about all your deficits. But if you try to get intimacy while solving pragmatic problems, you won't get any of it.

This is the kind of relationship garbage that fills our entire world. In such a situation, your intimacy will be in constant short supply, you will feel that you are denied it. And what do you want if you come in with a list of your inner tensions and overload?

It's very important to understand that even a professional therapist, if you go beyond the stresses that the session implies, will deny you some amount of intimacy, even though you buy it for money, and intimacy is the product you wish to purchase.

For example, you come to a therapy session and begin an endless monologue: "My mother is sick, and my daughter can't get a job. My granddaughter has diathesis and I have back pain. My friend is sick of me. I can't buy myself a new dress..." This flow does not allow you to go to the language of intimacy, because you go too far, do not feel the edge in time to stop.

So it's very important to find your deficits in time and differentiate. And if you want to figure out what you should do with your deficits, how to work with them, then buy a film. It's called *The Evolution of Needs*, and it tells how to deal with your needs, how to satisfy them, how to find people for that, how to be a quality consumer, in a good sense, of everything that the modern world offers, and feel that you are happy, fulfilled.

Intimacy and Death

I am often asked what to do with our intimacy energy after one partner dies. I can recommend Irvin Yalom's[14] book, *Staring at the Sun*, which talks about the soul's postmortem experience and preparation for the transition to another plane of being.

Each case is individual; it all depends on whether or not the intimacy between the souls has been preserved, which continues to provide them with a spiritual connection, because if there was no such intimacy during life, then two weeks after death, all of our love or kinship ties are annulled. They are simply erased and remain as a kind of experience that, in general, is no longer remembered, and which is not important to you on either side of reality.

---

14 Irvin David Yalom is an American psychotherapist, MD, professor of psychiatry at Stanford University. He was an opponent of the impersonal, formal approach to psychotherapy, the so-called 'short-term diagnosis-oriented therapy', which functioned on a commercial basis and was based on formal diagnoses, without regard for the individuality of the patient. Yalom advocated therapy built on an interpersonal (sincere and trusting) relationship between the patient and psychotherapist.

After forty days, you are permanently disconnected from your partner. Maybe there was a spiritual, emotional, and heartfelt intimacy between you during your lifetime, and you experienced a space of unity. Then this person, when they leave, becomes a guardian angel for you and provides your earthly path with their unconditional Divine love, and the connection between you is already beyond time and space. By this bond of intimacy, we find each other in the next lives.

Instincts

Why does intimacy have the incredible effect of melting space with itself? Why is it the alchemy of our soul and our spirit? Because intimacy is a quality of being of a soul, and when the space of intimacy is in act, a certain message of our soul is in act, too. And that's when the instincts go to sleep.

Humans have twelve basic instincts that govern their life activities on an unconditioned, unconscious level, and lurk in the most ancient parts of the brain. When mankind began to evolve as a species, instincts were at the heart of the process. All of them (territorial, food, sexual, gregarious and others) are necessary for a clear division according to the principle 'friend-or-foe'. Who is safe, who is dangerous?

People with an instinctive level of development of spiritual, emotional, psychological spheres get the world for themselves accordingly. They always fight on the level of instincts: who is ahead of whom, a stranger—a friend, a pack—not a pack, we protect our own, we kill strangers. They do not care about other people, other women, other children. They divide the world into their own and everything else. And this is where instinct helps the species to survive.

But we have evolved; we have matured higher mental functions, more complex mechanisms of being, allowing us to become higher than animals, to move from a state of survival to a state of prosperity.

We study trainings, meditation techniques, information from literary sources, and they all advocate this. "Limitless abundance, limitless possibilities! Visualise, imagine, be in the flow! There are billions of money on earth that is just lying in funds and not invested anywhere because there are no growing markets, no true entrepreneurs. It's all just in front of you, take it." But for some reason, it doesn't happen at the snap of a finger. And why, in fact?

Because as long as your psychic body operates on the level of instinct, you pose an unconscious danger to other living beings forced to interact with you on the same level.

We perceive by our animal part of the psyche that a survival-level interaction is about to take place: 'friend-or-foe'.

I. Me. Mine. My border, my territory, my life.

My instincts calm down as I begin to move into a state of intimacy with the world, and a philosophical idea first dawns on me: I and the world are one, God is within me, I am connected to another person, the whole world is connected by an invisible golden thread, we are all one. And this territory is spiritually higher, nobler, more generous, and richer.

Yes, it is the territory of other possibilities in terms of energy, love, relationships, everything that I dream of and that gives colour, flavour, beauty to life.

This philosophical, Buddhist idea, this religious message or just a psychological affirmation allows you to feel an intimacy with the whole world. You and the world are one. And so you will not be abandoned by God (or a 'higher reason' if you don't believe in God), or by some system that allows the planets to be held around the sun. This order, this discipline, this harmony exists.

The world is ingeniously organised and has a single energy, a single beginning, a single centre. And I am part of this space, I am included in it, it takes me into account. The sun knows that I am here, because its ray touched me. I thought about something, and an answer came to me, a response. I suddenly moved into a state in which I feel myself part of the universe. I suddenly realised that everything around me is alive, and that my soul is immortal.

Our animal part and our spiritual part exist in us simultaneously. We carry God and the Beast within us. The cross, in which the vertical rung is God and the horizontal rung is the Beast, is enclosed in our heart. Our instincts say, "Survive on your own, think for yourself, take care of your money, take care of your territory, take care of all that is yours. If you don't take care of yourself, no one will take care of you."

The soul objects, "If I don't love people, don't trust them, don't open up…If I don't take risks, don't let them come into my life and maybe break it and trample on my feelings, my heart, then I won't get this life. I will constantly be like a timid dear, guarding myself, and I will not know what God intended for me when He allowed me to come into the world." You begin to trust the world, and at that moment, on a psychological level, your instincts are weakened.

They no longer squeeze your throat, demanding that you survive at all costs, they no longer wake you up in the middle of the night to say, "What money will you live on tomorrow, how will you pay for your apartment, where, finally, is your man to protect your when you are old, take care of you, give you an offspring?."

Instincts are very strong, they are the base of our psyche, and a healthy psyche has strong instincts. But these same instincts turn you into a survival animal, a perpetually wary creature with high levels of adrenaline in your blood, with a sense of danger, with a sense that you need something from those around you. You cannot feel relaxed with them. You need them to work for their money.

You need them to justify this and that. You are in control of anything and everything, and you just can't be in a state of spontaneous creativity. After all, your instincts have overridden the higher mental compartments of your brain. Instincts determined the predominance of biochemical processes, which inject litres of adrenaline into your blood, making you sweat and shiver, raising your blood pressure and accumulating lactic acid in your muscles.

But! When you're in creation, in flux, when you take risks, open up, suddenly all these stress reactions go away.

Of course, it's very difficult to find that balance when your instincts are calm, peaceful, don't wake you up in the middle of the night, don't remind you of bills, appointments, outings. They talk about it, but quietly, on the periphery of consciousness, and your priority is trust, creativity. This state of intimacy with your life gives you a universal sense of relaxation.

You're relaxed, you're kind, you're creative and sensitive, you have a lot of free energy, free attention. And suddenly insights come, you are visited by genius ideas that give birth to abundance, demand, popularity.

And you realise that life is a gift, and you are in intimacy with everybody, you don't see them as a danger anymore, you find a common language with them every second. And if you see that they are traumatised, trapped, afraid, you let them go for a while. Maybe they'll come back, feeling that there was something magical here to learn.

Life flies by quickly, and if you constantly stop, reacting to every stone thrown, to every dog barking, to every negative situation, the path will remain unpassed. Let things happen, let dogs bark, let rocks fly, let it rain. The important thing is to come to the temple of your realisation, to fulfil your dreams, to reach where you destination.

And your instincts suddenly get calmed down, because they see that despite the craziness of everything going on around you, you are achieving a positive result.

But the result is unattainable without creativity, and creativity is impossible without relaxation. You will not come up with ingenious new tricks of working with clients, ingenious new algorithms and stunning outfit for business negotiations, if you will be strung out. On the contrary, in order to dress nicely, think through the nuances of behaviour, be in the flow (and those around you will definitely appreciate it), you need to be relaxed and calm, not waste energy fighting with life, and initially be in an intimate relationship with it.

Intimacy with Two Sexual Partners at the Same Time

A very important question is intimacy with two sexual partners possible at the same time.

You can't have one partner if some of your parts are not in intimacy with your psyche. If all the parts of your psyche are loved by you, you are aware of them, you have them integrated, you are in contact with them, then they are also aware of each other.

Let's say one of your parts is a little girl, who is waiting for some miracle or fairy tale, and beautiful events. Your other part is an aggressive lover, longing for passionate experiences. These two parts of the psyche may be in conflict because of different traumas.

For example, in the mother, her lover was in conflict with her inner girl, and so the loss of innocence was a certain traumatic experience that she did not fully comprehend and process. The daughter may also have a conflict of innocence and sexuality.

The two parts within you are dissociated, and you can include either one or the other. Innocence and, conventionally speaking, sexual emancipation are somehow difficult to connect; there is no dialogue between them, and then you lose intimacy with your sexual wholeness, and can only experience intimacy with some of your separate parts.

Since they cannot live in you at the same time, you begin to delegate them to different partners, and thus you are not entirely in intimacy with these partners. They are like different post offices for you, from which you send different mail.

Intimacy is a state of wholeness, and if some part of you is missing at the moment of contact with a person, it's because you are rejecting that part of yourself. You will attract a partner who is also not wholly in a relationship, who also lacks integrity. And if there is no wholeness, then some parts we don't like, we reject; they suffer, they are sick, they are in deficit.

Let's say some part of you is concerned about the state of your affairs (you're not dressed that way, or combed that way, or are recalling your conversation with your mother). In this situation, you cannot move into intimacy, you will remain in a relationship at the level of meeting psychological needs. And, accordingly, you will attract a partner who has the same psychological, spiritual assembly when he is one side with you and the other side somewhere else.

We always feel very clearly: the partner is with us entirely in the relationship, or some parts of them somewhere are in a state of satisfaction of needs, covering their deficits, in a state of internal conflict with you. These parts may not be nurtured, they are just children, and they are afraid of something inside us—the person in some issues has not matured spiritually or emotionally yet.

There are many reasons why certain fragments of the psyche are not in touch with the soul. The state of intimacy occurs when all internal parts, thoughts, feelings, sub-personalities, connections with the external world (i.e., all your role models of life) have a rapport with the soul. When the soul accepts them all, having free access to this world through any of your role models.

This is the very result, the very spiritual, psychological, emotional goal that we set for ourselves when we start working with this topic, to answer the question: why is it all necessary on the level of higher meaning? Why did God design it this way? Why such a gradation in relationships, and such a hierarchy, and such plans?

In the beginning, we are at the level of deficit, in our childlike state, and we cannot live without someone, and we need someone badly. And our survival is tied to that person, compensating for some of our very deficit states.

Then we move to a higher level of needs, when we can choose how to satisfy ourselves, what we have a request for, what develops us, fills us, moves us forward.

Imagine that there is a deficit of cleanliness in the apartment. It's a pretty tough deficit, and it's necessary to put everything in order. And you usually invite people to do this who themselves live in deficits, for whom earning from your apartment is not something out of a sense of intimacy with your apartment, but a way to cover their own deficits.

All right, that deficit is closed, and, having barely begun to arise, is already closed on schedule. Let's say every Thursday either your in-house part, or a specialist who comes to you provides coverage for this deficit, and it ceases to be acute. As it accumulates, it is removed, so to speak, in a workman-like manner.

Now you go to the needs and say, "Ah, my place is clean, but I want it to be nicer. I'll buy flowers, order interior decoration, invite friends." You have a need, something that can diversify and beautify your life. It is the same in communication with people: you understand that you do not just need a friend, like Robinson Crusoe, at least someone to talk to.

No, you need someone who, for example, understands what impressionism is or is interested in the history of fashion. Or maybe you need someone who is interested in self-development. You start looking for that circle of people and it's those with whom you have a closing relationship, and they're usually at that same stage of development themselves.

And so, when all of life's necessary needs are met, you feel better about yourself. You are relaxed, you begin to experience abundance; you basically have no psychological hunger, no feeling of not being cuddled. And you can pick up a sexual partner or 'life partner' on the level of need. Why is it often said that marriages of convenience are the strongest? Because if you yourself have grown to the level of your needs, you should choose your partner at the same level.

The next, even higher bar is a relationship of intimacy, when our needs are met, we have accumulated the experience of satiation.

We all dream of a magical state of intimacy. It is told about in fairy tales, we have once experienced it. It gives an incredible sense of soul-filling life, and you feel God within you when you experience this intimacy.

We often idealise this state, see it as a very high bar. We necessarily want to experience it, and if it's not with a partner, "...then maybe it's not quite my partner. And I will still wait for the one with whom I will have exactly this experience, this state."

This idealisation of intimacy is detrimental to personal life, to the psyche, to a woman's self-esteem, to looking clearly at life and really addressing the issue of self-filling. Instead of fantasising, it is always more helpful to have your own psychological plan.

Yes, intimacy, indeed, is a very high bar of human mental development, and the state of intimacy is a divine gift of a working heart, a living soul. In order to reach this level of union with your partner, you have to have and know your basic needs. You need to be able to close them with those ordinary people who live in your city, neighbourhood, driveway.

Who went to the same school with you, or with whom you work together. From the perspective of the divine plan, all the people given to you for a relationship are within reach.

Our soul longs for intimacy so much that this longing accumulates in the form of tremendous heartache. We begin to divide everything into this trauma without adequately assessing what, in fact, there is a need for. For sex, for tactile sensations, for going on vacation with the right person for me. To have someone to take care of me morally and physically. And I myself feel the need to take care of someone…

But here is the level of our needs closed, we have learned to deal with it. Once a woman or man is able to fill themselves psychologically at the level of need, they naturally find themselves in the next stage of development. There is no need to dream about it, perform pretentious magical rituals or climb Mount Everest.

We are all moving upward in the spiral of evolution. When you've covered your deficits, met your needs, your psyche will be ready to open up moments of intimacy either with your current partner or, if it hasn't moved to that level, with a partner who will definitely show up in your life and give it to you. They simply appear in front of you, and you actually experience with them this experience, which, of course, all books, all fairy tales describe as the apogee of earthly existence.

But it was not romantic love, not finding a partner, not creating a family that the great artists, writers and poets described when they praised the union of woman and man as the highest meaning of life. They worshipped the state of intimacy, meaning that you let God into your soul, you see God in the other person, and you connect with the entire universe and create for yourself a field of all-acceptance, all-disclosure, kindness and the realisation of your spirit.

And so your heart and soul (the shell for spirit, the channel for your immortal part to descend into your consciousness and begin to interact with your psyche) are initiated through intimacy with others. At this point, a spiritual, sacred marriage occurs—the union of your spirit and soul.

This path lies through the fact that you, having satisfied your needs, learn to build a relationship of intimacy with people. No matter how many incarnations you are destined to, in each of them you will follow the evolution of the law of intimacy, and each time in order to reach your new stage of development you will fly to this light and give your life to get this experience. And the people who bring it into your life are marked by God, and those relationships are holy.

Those who experience deep intimacy with those around them in life have a very special, luminous soul, a very different capacity that the immortal spirit carries within them.

L. N. Tolstoy's book *Father Sergius* tells of how a man on the path of spiritual search, very persistently yearned for holiness, enlightenment, and ascension. In the end, he saw holiness in a woman who was in the deepest intimacy with herself, with life, with loved ones, with relatives. His experience corresponds exactly to what I am telling you now.

Intimacy with others, acceptance of life, the energy of connection with others at the level of an unconditional state of intimacy are closely related to the realisation of the immortal soul, the immortal spirit, and ultimately the state of holiness. I recommend paying attention to the way in which the protagonist of this book realises that without intimacy, without its energy, there is no spiritual path as such.

You are motivated for intimacy not only to realise yourself in your personal life, to resolve conflicts, or to get out of difficult karmic scenarios. Your desire has to do with the fact that throughout your incarnations, you are seeking the tools to heal your heart and soul for intimacy because that is the channel of entry into our divine consciousness and into our lives as supreme immortal creatures of the Creator.

The soul trembles when you realise the degree of importance of the process, and stop using other people to fill your life. And, if you do use, by making an honest, win-win deal, giving your partner what he or she needs.

Please meet your needs, don't live as a victim who lacks tenderness, tactile contact, warmth, travel, and gifts. Be active, act, and don't think that by doing so you are tarnishing the great longing for intimacy, for complete unity, for the purity and beauty of relationships. In the dynamics of evolution, at some point in your life, you may have parallel partners for your needs, and in this situation don't be frustrated by the fact that there is no intimacy with them.

After all, they may have been given to you for something else. And if you have more than one partner, it's probably an indication that you're working on integrating your psycho-emotional parts.

So intimacy with two sexual partners at the same time is difficult for itself initially. Can I be intimate with myself when the parts of my psyche are so separate? It's probably very difficult for me to hold on to the intimacy channel myself, to hold on to my inner wholeness. And I try, attracting the energy of other people to karmically work through this, to get over it, to take on such hard work—to keep two men in my space.

And at this point, if I'm not completely in intimacy with myself, and I'm just trying to resolve this issue, will I be able to give that intimacy to two people? And will those partners who are ready to be wholly in that relationship be attracted to a sexual role model that is not fully intimate? Do they themselves have all their parts integrated? If not, then the needs are not closed.

But do these 'men as wise as Solomon' who have all their needs closed really exist? Yes, there do. Especially since satisfaction in needs may not necessarily be a permanent, stable personality quality, but a state in which a person wished to do so and began to 'assemble' himself. And a perfectly ordinary, simple man, who has never heard the terms 'higher self' and 'needs', really wants to be a husband.

His astrological readings, his consciousness of intention, his inner role model merged into a desire to be a husband. All this quickly gathers and binds all the other parts of his psyche together in this volitional intention, choice of purpose, decision making.

Men often come to me for counselling with this wholeness, intimacy with themselves. Everything begins to organise, if only for the intention. Here he becomes a husband, and all the painful parts come to this strong central assembly point, which is the most important in his life right now. The sick boy, the frustrated lover, the fractured entrepreneur adjoin the husband, and he leads them all.

In this state of wholeness, he is really close to his wife. At the wedding, he is all with her, all in the church. Nothing within him argues, nothing conflicts; he is close to God and in intimacy with himself.

It turns out that there can be more than one partner to meet different needs and deficits. But I remind you, as always, that it is easier to heal the karmic knots of a relationship by going through everything well, beautifully, and leaving no loose ends behind. But if you, for example, start infringing on your partner's needs, you will, on the contrary, create karmic debts to him or her.

Thus, you should critically assess the status of your relationships and understand how many deficits are there, how many needs are there, and how much of intimacy.

And the very game with the man must be honest. Unfortunately, women are very prone to manipulation. They portray intimacy, they want it, they themselves close off needs and deficits and complain that they have no intimacy, that their soul groans and suffers in this relationship. That they, after all, don't feel full disclosure in the relationship.

"How could this ever happen? Why is my soul not soaring, not flying, but as if it were nailed to the marital bed?." Soul and heart are indeed crying, tearing and clobbering at the feeling that they can't live without intimacy.

But please don't lie to yourself and substitute concepts.

What were you in this relationship for, and what was your inner intention in choosing this partner? You didn't choose him out of intimacy ("so that he is here, and my soul would perceive him, soar and be happy")? Then don't expect that after two years of relationship, you will suddenly come out to intimacy through needs.

After all, he didn't go to that level of development either, he didn't have those vibes, but he had the need to get married, build a relationship, a family, a home. He was solving these issues equally with you, everything was fair.

But now you, as the keeper of life, suddenly panic and want to make up for the time. "God, I haven't lived through something so very important; something goes away, God, where is it, how?." Time falls through your fingers like sand, and you realise: it turns out that intimacy has tremendous value, but the culture to approach it isn't there.

And there is no understanding of why you haven't approached it. Awareness of how it all works, and the ability to differentiate between different kinds of relationships is also missing. Therefore, it is very important to make and implement a plan for mental, emotional development as early as possible.

Competition for Intimacy

All of this is a philosophy of being from the quality of intimacy. But theory, as you remember, does not exist without practice, so pay attention to the very important technique 'Competition for intimacy'. It can be an indispensable aid if intimacy in the heart, intimacy with life, interaction with others through the energy of intimacy has weakened.

Little things can happen. During a physical ailment, for example, it is difficult to hold intimacy even with one's own body because it suffers. This reduces the level of trust in the world and in life, because the body may signal that it is barely alive, and this will awaken survival instincts. There is no room for creative flight or the intimacy of being.

All sorts of circumstances in life can 'slow you down'. And you will feel that it is necessary to build up the environment of intimacy, to search for new partners or new resources, to work out for yourself a new fabric of life. And you find yourself in an environment where people compete for intimacy based on animal instincts. That's why we are so reserved.

We, those who have success, prosperity, money, don't really want any new contacts. At the same time, we live in a field where people compete for intimacy as a resource, gnawing it out based on our animal instincts. But that's not how intimacy works. Competition for it exists, but it must stem from other considerations. Not in order to survive, but in order to secure intimacy for its own sake.

Competition for intimacy from animal instincts means that people want intimacy with other people in order to have more love, more money, all the things that intimacy is not.

Intimacy is self-sufficient; it is a resource in its own right, for which you must compete from a state of intimacy, not instinctively, with those you like. Win back the space of intimacy for yourself in their hearts so that you have a special relationship with them, a spiritual and soul base resource.

You want to be healthy—compete for intimacy, build, no matter what, relationships with those people you like and feel you value intimacy with them as such. You really want to see that these people like you, you really want to have the right to send them a gift for the New Year and to receive a gift from them, too. You feel that the very familiarity with this person gives you strength.

Somehow the intimacy with them is a kind of creative impetus for you. Compete for that intimacy from a state of mind, build golden bridges for yourself; don't be left out, because if you don't provide yourself with this basic resource, no one will come to you and say, "Oh, I've been looking for you all my life, you and I are going to be incredibly close now, I feel this spontaneous intimacy."

There are no such miracles. You can experience that intimacy with a therapist for money, yes. But for the rest, you have to arrange it for yourself.

Here's a little exercise. Try to answer the questions honestly.

What kinds of people do you like very much?

How many people in your life with whom you—of those you like—are really close?

Who would you like to be close to?

Think of everyone, from politicians to actors. Try to interact with yourself and answer yourself, who would you like to be intimate with, who do you really like, is there enough of that intimacy in your life? What kind of intimacy do you really lack, and why aren't you competing for it, why aren't you putting your mental resources into surrounding yourself with the kind of intimacy that would be as pure, transparent, and beautiful as spring water?

In the realm of instincts, we survive on the level of basic resources, but in the realm of the soul, we survive on intangible resources, and through the fact that we are constantly changing. By competing for intimacy with those we like, we abandon false pride, we are willing to soulfully adjust ourselves to the person and admit to ourselves that their energy and attention are very important to us; without contact with their soul we have no way forward.

You could call it the art of soulful romance, which keeps us 'in the forefront', makes us emotionally fulfilled, in love with this life and with these people. It's the kind of state in which there are a little more endorphins in the blood than it takes just to find the strength to live. It is the inspiration that the person has opened their soul, told everything about themselves, showed their life, shared something innermost.

Life brings us together with unique, amazing people, from whose hands, hearts, souls we learn the mysteries of God. We stay in this state, and our endorphin levels are such that in the morning we bounce around like a volleyball. We are overflowing with creative energy, enthusiasm, we have the desire to do sports or yoga, to call our mother, to plant a tree, to throw out junk from the apartment, to have sex. We suddenly become wizards and creators.

But we draw this enthusiasm from our soulful romance, and it is very important to compete on a soul level with ourselves. It is on the animal level that competition is with others, based on instincts that divide the world into 'friend' and 'foe', allowing us to survive and compete for resources.

And by competing with ourselves to nurture high mental qualities, putting away our pride, forgetting what a 'traumatised centre of the earth' we are, coming out of our incomplexity, we say, "God, at the cost of my life, I am now ready to wait for this person to pay attention to me."

Such competition for intimacy has no negative connotations for highly intelligent, advanced people who are scrupulous about their vibrations, spirituality, and ethical standards, competition that appeals to ourselves.

You are competing with your complexes, your pride, your traumas, your deficits; you are competing for the best mental qualities within yourself, and so you get into the spiritual space, you are doing the inner work to enter into a relationship of intimacy with a certain person. And, if at that point you get into an environment where other men or women are competing for that same person, you will be at an advantage.

You will suddenly see that you are ahead of them all, acting on the level of animal instincts, because you are sincere, there is warmth coming from you.

There have been many wonderful cases in my life, when I got unique connections and acquaintances at big events—forums, symposiums, summits. Out of all the huge mass of people—spectacular, bright, smart—necessarily there was a person who for some reason had a desire to sit down next to me, talk, get acquainted, talk to each other. Something drew them in, like a magnet.

It's the heart that attracts. You suddenly realise in your heart that, one way or another, you will reach intimacy with the one you like.

You don't settle for psychological scraps of communication in a space in which nothing inspires you. In a space in which contact with that person's soul will be an incurable trauma for you for the next fifteen years. It will be terrible for you, you are not ready, you do not want to, you have the right to choose, you are competing in this world for the quality of intimacy.

Competition is selection. And when it starts to happen within you, when you choose to win for yourself, then winning becomes the quality of energy in which you will become living. For me, for example, it's how I'm going to spend the last twenty years of my life, and during that period, all what is left is to talk. And it's very important to me who I'm going to visit on my 70th birthday, having packed my bags to go across the world for my birthday.

Who planted in me this seed of happiness, this unique experience of romance? How did my heart struggle to build a golden bridge and connect with them in that quality of intimacy and togetherness that gives me wings? I see that these people have accepted me for who I am, there is sympathy between us, we feel each other and we have created our common field, a 'we' space into which the energy of the world has flowed.

If you are in a 'we' with someone out of intimacy, you feel that in that moment everything in the world favours you. The wine takes on an extraordinary flavour. You are good-looking, and men pay attention to you. You like your clothes. Your body experiences tenderness, and your soul is open to the world, because through 'we' with one person in intimacy, you discover the universe in intimacy with God, with all that surrounds us.

The energy of 'we' includes 'we' with God, with life's perspectives, with those people you haven't met yet, but in twenty years, you certainly will. I never thought, for example, that I would have dinner or lunch with a very large number of famous people who were simply interesting to me out of intimacy, out of the soul. But there are so many of these pictures in my photo album, and there are so many gifts in my house that are made by these people.

The unique quality of being in intimacy is, of course, necessary in any profession, because you begin to weave social space, to create society and the world of relationships, rather than trying to do this or that manipulation.

Here is an important exercise. Imagine that in front of you is a space of intimacy with everyone you like: your potential men, potential girlfriends, business partners, investors or relatives with whom you want to be intimate, and even your unborn children and grandchildren. This space fills you with inspiration, you live with these people in unconditional harmony.

Imagine that all this space is in front of you, you see it quite clearly. Listen to your heart now, feel how big the distance is between you and this future. What lies between you and the space of intimacy? Is it resentment, trauma, broken relationships, failures, disappointments, fears, emotions? Maybe the other person's rejection of intimacy?

Try to make a list or picture for yourself: what lies between you and your intimacy space. Believe me, you are already on your way to insights, revelations, and changes in the quality of your life, your consciousness on the most concrete, practical level.

As they say, the most important and meaningful documents must rest. Let them spend the night in your desk, and at night your subconsciousness will unload files from your psyche with information about what stands between you and true intimacy, so that you get more information and complete this list.

Trauma, Evolution, Points and Deficits of Intimacy

Let's now move on to the next important topic that helps to map out the vectors of our intimacy.

Excercise

The exercise is called 'My Personal Vectors of Intimacy'.
Divide the sheet of paper into four parts.
In the centre of the sheet, write 'Intimacy'.
At the top left, write 'Intimacy Traumas'.
Top right: 'The Evolution of Intimacy'.
Bottom left: 'Points of Real Intimacy in my Life'.
Bottom right: 'Intimacy Deficits in My Life'.
Start to fill out the worksheet.
'Intimacy Traumas'.

For example, I don't know where I'm coming from, but I have a fear of going into intimacy, a lack of energy, insecurity. I have no experience of building intimacy with any person, on all levels.

And yet the skills of building intimacy are wonderful in that they spontaneously arise with people of all ethnicities, confessions, ages and languages, and with any attitude towards you. If you begin to interact with this energy, it automatically becomes a universal way of dialogue with the whole world. Among the traumas of intimacy, you will list perhaps those that stand between you and intimacy in the previous exercise.

'The Evolution of Intimacy'.

These are your expectations of intimacy, its evolution in your life, its perspective. Perhaps you would like intimacy to connect with love or with faith in God. Perhaps you would deepen this lake and have underground springs in it; perhaps you don't have enough space, you want more people or more transparency. Or you want healing of some relationship in intimacy with specific people, and those people, let's say, you have in your mind right now.

Maybe they're alive, maybe they're dead—that happens too. In the evolution of intimacy, write out the things that are really important to your realisation.

"Points of Real Intimacy in my Life."

With whom and what kind of intimacy do you think you have? Try to differentiate, for example, spiritual, sexual, relational intimacy. And with someone, intimacy can be...negative.

So what is negative intimacy, and how does it arise in our lives?

Unfortunately, we live in a society in which very often people see intimacy as a field of suffering. For example, children very often lack attention and struggle for it. They know that when they are unhappy (sick or having a fight with someone), attention is guaranteed to them. Moreover, they see that in the family, if adults fight, they often give each other intimacy.

Indeed, when we fight, get irritated, take something personally, we form a bond between intimacy and negativity. A program is fixed in us: to be in an argument, in confrontation, in negativity, in suffering, is to be in intimacy. You would be surprised, but for 80 per cent of all people, being in intimacy means being in a problematic, very difficult relationship.

Especially this statistic concerns men, who very often, not having the skills to build intimacy and not having the ability to get it from a woman, start to make mistakes at work, talk about lack of money and even 'go off the rails'. This is how they get attention, attract energy to get intimacy in the usual way. And they love to bathe in our intimacy, and for them, it is just as important, if not more, than sex.

They are after our intimacy. Where do we look; how do we feel about them; what mood are we in; what are we dressed up for? They're watching where our intimacy energy has flowed to control it; it's a stress point for them.

Therefore, I often don't take people to my programs, trainings, counselling sessions whose intimacy script is 100 per cent negativity and suffering. They are bound to start conflicts, provoke confrontation, and deliberately reduce the significance of events. They will manipulate, feel uncomfortable emotions. After all, in order to form an open intimacy in love, they have no language, no state of mind, no faith.

But this is still intimacy, even though it is negative. People provoke you to it, to some stress, to some additional points of attention, points of tension, because that is their language of intimacy. And they get it, like when you were a kid, by breaking your knee.

"We're close to you in this moment, Mom. I'm bleeding, I'm in pain. You hold me, you kiss me, you forget about pans, dresses, movies, husband, mother-in-law, the store. You have forgotten everything, you are all with me now. And I feel it as one, *we*." I have a program written down: intimacy is broken knees. And one calms down by saturating oneself with negative intimacy.

These forms of negative intimacy repel some of you. You feel that you will meet exclusively with negativity, which the person will begin to unwind. And, when they sense that you are not going for this kind of intimacy, they will take it as the deepest insult, the worst thing you could do.

They will never forgive you because we all live in a deficit of intimacy, and that defines, in today's society, connections, resources, and therefore, its entire future. So many simply don't have the competence to build harmonious intimacy, they don't have that ecology of the soul.

And suddenly, on this desolate, bare rock, someone appears who clearly has this ecology in abundance, who competes for positive intimacy with the world, with space, with themselves. Who is warm, happy, filled and exchanging delicious, beautiful energy with the world. And you glide in a stream of love, acceptance, kind relationships, signs of attention.

And it's all very ecological, and you understand how it all works. You will not abuse that knowledge. On the contrary, you will make an effort to heal your negative forms of intimacy, you will try to realise which ones you 'rise' to, and how you can be manipulated.

The subtle body of the soul is nourished by positive intimacy, saturated with it, living, flourishing. On the contrary, any negative form, like poison, destroys it. It instantly penetrates into the subtle structure of our psyche and causes us sometimes very serious, deep harm, the consequences of which we have to get rid of for a long time afterwards.

All resentments, all relationship breakups, all forms of revenge and slander have at their core a huge lack of intimacy, an inability to exchange it, and the tendency of someone involved in the process to develop the relationship in a negative way.

Try to recognise 'from the get-go' those who have an addiction to a negative form of intimacy, because these are psychological strategies that are very close to addiction in level of tension. Intimacy is a basic resource, and if you don't have it, you have all kinds of psychological processes broken. When you deny a person who is experiencing intimacy deficits, they do not realise that you are simply not willing to go for negative intimacy.

Virtually, all murders, stalking, property grabbing, and child abduction involve revenge for the pain of not receiving intimacy. It really is a tremendous and harshly scarce resource. And revenge, and persecution, and slander will have no limit because the war over the resource of intimacy is the endless psychological warfare of our era.

Most of the time a person is unable to believe that they do not have to fight, to accuse, to suspect, to snatch their own. That everything they need, they will get in time, and everything will be fine. Alas, they will still engage in a brutal emotional scramble to gain a place in your space by any means necessary, to wrest a piece of intimacy from your heart.

Negative energy is energy, too. At least some energy is better than none. And, if a person has no choice, or doesn't know how to differentiate between these states, or doesn't have the multiple sources of intimacy in their life worked out...Or their partners pull them into negative intimacy relationships, or they have some form of co-dependency from it or a traumatic attachment to negative intimacy, then they will draw negative energy from it.

Why do people provoke us to negative intimacy through suffering, complaining, sharing negative information, fighting, prolonged conflict, ignoring, hidden aggression, silent rejection? To get that negative energy.

And yet intimacy is a digital code to our subconscious, to our soul, to the deeper aspects of our psyche. It is the 'lubricant' for the functioning of our entire inner psycho-emotional structure. Everything you receive straight from intimacy directly affects your subconscious mind, life program, unconscious choices, health, relationships with loved ones and personal relationships.

When you enter negative intimacy, you are giving negative programs the keys to your apartment, to your inner world, to your psyche, to the way you will live out your future. You allow these negative programs to plan and determine your being.

Intimacy is water, which, whether clean or dirty, is instantly absorbed, and permeates our lives. Intimacy is a state of increased psychological permeability. You can't do without it, but if you allow negative intimacy in psychohygiene, then be ready for your subconsciousness to be overloaded with negative programs coming from unconscious generic attitudes, past traumas, current fears and stresses.

This negative energy has the same power, the same potential as the positive energy, only their vectors are different. But both of them are energetic messages that give an impulse to move, live, and create.

Sometimes it seems to us that we can achieve even better results with negative energy, because now we will achieve balance, try to balance negative events with some positive actions. Conventionally speaking, you had a fight with your girlfriend—you went through your entire closet; you had a fight with your husband—you finally got together for fitness; you had a fight with your child—you finally managed to sort out your old library.

But in this way, you get addicted to negative energy, and it's very hard to switch to a positive channel of intimacy after that. You don't get into it on a vibration level and stop attracting people and circumstances that carry positive energy. Especially when you consider that positive intimacy in this world is in great short supply, and of course, those who have it in their lives will guard their private space with special care, with special love.

It is not easy to then fit into the circle of positive companionship, but it is very easy to get out of it, and that is the reason why negative intimacy is so common. But please, do not confuse negative intimacy with resistance to intimacy; these are completely different phenomena that must be clearly differentiated.

Negative intimacy is easier to give and more prevalent than positive intimacy. Negative intimacy is also intimacy, and the psyche recognises it as a form of acceptance, empathy. After all, if the person has taken my suffering seriously and entered into a struggle or conflict with me, it means that they have noticed me, I am included in their world, we are one in this negative energy.

And from there, it's as if a golden grain of 'me and you, we are one' is taken out for the psyche. 'We' is still created, only on a negative ground, an entirely different ground from the one on which people create 'we' on the basis of creativity.

'Intimacy Deficits in my Life'.

Where does it hurt? I want to be hugged warmly by a man, I miss that. My mother is dead, and I miss intimacy with her so much. I haven't had children, I long for the feeling of motherhood. Or I have a child, but we have no intimacy. Or I have it, but it's not of the quality I'd like.

These intimacy deficits also occur when you have an impulse to open up, and the energy comes back if the person doesn't accept it. It's a blow to the heart, to the soul, and you feel very intense pain. Your energy comes back and it has to go out into the world. We feel happy when we give and the world receives. Then we are liberated and given new strength.

But, if you send an impulse of intimacy and the person gives it back, you form a sense of deficit; a shared space of 'we' has not emerged. And sometimes we make our own mistakes, quit, break up. Perhaps you lack yourself to be close to the whole world and feel an intimacy with the space.

'Be like children' is about as if you have no trauma or resistance under your belt; you smile, you are open, you are simple. And, if it misleads anyone, that's the choice of the person next to you.

So why do we have such a shortage of a state of intimacy? Because most people are not connected to their needs, don't know how to meet them, have deficits, and try to get those need-related resources from each other. Our psyche shuts down in response, and we don't give each other heartfelt intimacy because when we meet needs, the psyche is regulated by instincts that block the intimacy channel.

Imagine how many people are so good at closing their deficits, so good at living, at filling themselves with all the necessary aspects that they have as internal tasks in life, that they don't bring them into your shared 'we' space. Where people meet their needs, there is a relationship of social partnership. But the spiritual, emotional, sensual intimacy is not there.

If a woman goes into a relationship out of a need to get married, to get herself a man, to establish her living space or to find a sponsor or someone to support her, don't expect intimacy in that relationship.

Because intimacy is when you have all these needs closed, and you are interested in the person himself by his quality of being. The soul feels this very clearly. The person is empty and opened up to me because I am me; he also offered himself to me, and this is the highest, stunning, incredible gift, this is divine music of the soul, this is the highest spiritual psychology.

A state where everything is beautiful, sublime, incredible, but has nothing to do with your dream of having someone to spend time with you when you are old.

That doesn't mean you can't look for someone to close your needs, please, do all you want, look for someone whose needs match yours. Perhaps by meeting them, you'll move on to intimacy. But more often than not, needs are still an issue that you must learn to solve for yourself, and intimacy is the state into which you move when your basic life deficits are closed.

Moving into Intimacy from the Needs Zone

Is it possible to move from needs to intimacy with the same person? You can if that person has a culture of meeting their needs.

If you entered into a relationship out of motivation to meet your needs, it's likely that's exactly the same reason that person showed up next to you. It is unlikely that you, a developing, seeking person, will be given a person who already has the potential for intimacy. As long as you fulfil your needs with someone, he or she will be in an intimacy relationship with someone. And then when you outgrow your level of needs, you will have them closed, you will be ready for intimacy with them.

Or you can, for example, just learn to take it beautifully, and it just stops bothering you because you know how to ask for a gift, how to ask your partner for your need. It becomes your current skill and you don't need to mobilise yourself anymore, you've evolutionarily outgrown that issue.

The strategies by which you move out of the need zone and into the intimacy space can be different. Most likely, a person who is capable of intimacy will tap into this energy potential. This energy is very scarce, and God wants it to 'not be idle'. In the pot of our life, everything moves, everything is boiled, everything must be demanded and realised.

And if there are some accumulated vibrational qualities in people, they will be realised in life as already working manifested scenario.

So if a person has intimacy potential, and you were with them out of need, they won't go for a relationship. But when you, having satisfied your needs with someone, move into a phase of intimacy, then in the next phase you connect with someone who is initially already attuned to that potential. They may come out of their previous relationship for the reason that they need a new vibration of intimacy.

And depending on what vibration you have awakened in yourself, what kind of intimacy you are ready for, comes just the one with whom everything is realised.

Ideally, we satisfy deficits first. We get married in our 20s with acute boy-girl deficits, and we all want to experience and learn it. Then we move on to the needs of making a nest, having children, building a world together. And after 45, we move on to intimacy because our needs are all closed and we are able to experience that state.

In fact, some of us develop so intensely that we sometimes realise all three plans in parallel. It happens so that a certain super-task appears, and not only deficits, necessity and intimacy have to be worked through, but also some karmic debts have to be closed. And, very often, with one partner you close karmic debts, and with the other you work through either need or intimacy. And time speeds up, squeezes, and hurries your evolution.

For those who work out these evolutionary qualities, a great many opportunities are thrown into space. And the most valuable of these is to enter into intimacy.

Intimacy Therapy

When you've sorted out your needs, you become ready for intimacy. Collapse happens if there's a huge list of unmet needs and you want more intimacy. And you try to combine both in space and time (for example, to do manicure, and unload all the problems to the unfortunate manicurist). But you should remember that everything that you give in space that is not ecological, in the same form will be received back.

You don't want clients, partners, girlfriends and husbands who will blow your mind with their negativity, their difficulties—don't dump it on other people but look at what need is behind it, find an ecological way to satisfy it and don't clog up the clean channels of intimacy with needs.

Because for qualitative needs, the situation is such that you can easily, technically, find the right tools for them, while intimacy is a more subtle form of the evolutionary state of consciousness, it's a completely different topic. When you confuse the two, you get neither. The person who is open to you for intimacy will feel very quickly if you try to use it pragmatically, and will not open their heart to you.

A young girl comes to me for counselling. I am in a basic state of intimacy, openness, acceptance, a state of oneness and a willingness to create a common 'we' with her. I see that she has come to satisfy a desperate curiosity about me personally. She's looking at everything, she's interested in every detail; she has a need to collect information. She doesn't care about intimacy with me; she doesn't create a shared 'we' space, she's struggling with her fears, calculating her money.

She's evaluating me; she's trying to gather material about what I'm like; what she can get here; how I feel about her. These are her needs; she doesn't know how to be alone with them. She energetically—in her thoughts, in her feelings, in her actions—pours them out into our shared space. At that point, my intimacy closes because it's a very heavy energy for the heart, not ecological.

It's not like I'm trying to make a client out of her at any cost or get her into some kind of scheme. I'm just trying to build a common 'we' with her so that we can have an alliance.

One of the spiritual teachers said that we all really want to do a job but we don't want to build a relationship. And until we have a relationship built, work remains a very difficult issue. Many conflicts and difficulties arise when we have to go to strangers, see them, work with them, and there are constantly strangers around us. A terrible strain on the psyche, which is not programmed for it.

The abundance of new people, their concepts of life, worldviews, habits, with the advent of the Internet and the possibility to instantly overcome distances, has turned into a huge flow, to which our psyche is not adapted.

There are many strangers around, who don't like you, who want to destroy you, who want to force you out of their space. Your psyche, selfish in a good way, is against it, it powerfully resists the hardest burden of seeing a new stranger. That's fine. But if you learn to meet your needs, learn to create your own circle of intimacy, there will be fewer strangers.

And your psyche will feel that even if they appear, you are ecologically protected from them by your close circle of communication.

But is it necessary to explain to those around you that you are not a bitch, and you just won't treat their deficits? Yes, it's very hard to endure the pressure of society, which is trying to wrest recognition and acceptance from you, including through negative intimacy. Yes, you can't be nice to everyone. There is one very simple way to be at peace with your soul and with your conscience.

Always start a relationship out of intimacy, out of a willingness to create a 'we'. Give everyone this chance, always be empty, always be pure, always be able to separate the needs and the state of intimacy, don't let yourself go, don't live in deficits. Be clear about your needs, meet them in time, so that everyone with whom you meet, in one way or another, is given a chance for intimacy.

After all, it may turn out to be a person who either has the gift of such intimacy by nature, or they are ready to go for it, or it is your soulmate who has met you in order to connect.

As a rule, approximately one person out of 15 goes spontaneously and naturally into intimacy, but this one is worth it to calmly endure the emotional revenge of those who did not go into intimacy with you. And, accordingly, just designate the situation, designate your boundaries in such a way that you are very benevolent, you are open, you are always ready to help, always be the one who demonstrates the principle of cooperation in any case.

And don't tease people with your inner state of peace and happiness, just be careful. Your main task is to give a chance in the beginning, and then not to allow yourself to be drawn into a negative intimacy.

And, if the person initially did not take advantage of this chance to build intimacy with you—does not have this competence, intuition, did not discern, did not see you as a diamond, which is valuable in itself, then they have looked at you through the prism of their deficits and needs. "What can this person give me? This is what I can learn from them, and I don't need this."

The person has crossed you off the intimacy list by their choice. Respect this right of people not to choose you for intimacy, but also ask them to respect within themselves that you are not willing to engage in negative intimacy and endlessly discuss difficult moments of being.

Protecting Intimacy

How do you properly protect existing intimacy, and do you need to protect it?

Since there is a great lack of energy for intimacy, it is true that when there is intimacy between someone, the world around them goes into a very nervous state. Everyone gets very nervous about it. People have a global deficit, and suddenly there is intimacy in some space. This attracts a great deal of aggression from the world around us because people want to get involved; everyone suddenly needs to talk about it, to poke a finger, to discuss, to touch.

This is why there are rites such as marriage, for example, and other sacred sacraments, where people invite God as third, and out of intimacy with themselves enter into an intimate relationship with God. Of course, this is a strong defence of intimacy, if it was there. Marriage on the level of need is just a beautiful ritual. But when there is intimacy between the partners, then marriage becomes something that protects it.

I must add here that in all religions and traditions, it is unacceptable to show one's feelings to others. It is indecent to embrace and kiss, so that the energy of intimacy will not arouse enemies around you.

If you have intimacy with yourself, the effect will be about the same: you will become a victim of other people's aggression. You will be seen as a source of this energy, and they will try to provoke negative intimacy in order to lower the vibration of pure intimacy, and then, to receive and digest this energy. In order to digest it, you have to do something so that the vibration within the couple or within the person is lowered.

Then you can talk to the person about how they're feeling, access that space under the guise of support and friendship. And the energy of intimacy will flow out of your soul like blood, and you'll feel a deep wound within you.

But the thing is, this stage is necessary until intimacy becomes your way of life. You will still go through this painful journey because if at this point you close your heart and start saving it, then you will not be out of intimacy with this world and not out of intimacy with God.

In a sense, you have to make sacrifices to space, and understand that when your intimacy becomes absolutely stable with yourself and your partner, you will have a sacred marriage phase. You will be wedded to God within your soul, and intimacy will be your light-bearing beginning. You will go through all the trials, all the provocations and greed of those around you for your inner energy of intimacy.

Taking advantage of you financially, materially, organisationally, whatever—it is really a desire to get your source of intimacy by taking either money, or time, or energy from you. It is simply an attraction to a person who has a resource of intimacy with God and with the world—a resource of abundant goodness that never ends.

And, in keeping with that, all those who are in short supply or need will come into your life to take something away from you. This is all done within the law of equilibrium, for you too were once evolutionarily raised and were a nobody, and out of ignorance, out of scarcity took something from someone.

Then your time has come to live in abundance, and you just pay it off, losing some resources, paying off debts. And now people with deficits or sick needs appear near you. They take from you a part of your life energy in the form of money, time, attention…

The process will stop when you become entrenched in this energy, which will become part of your global life choices, at which point this whole story will end because it will no longer be possible to vibrationally reach you on all levels. Life will begin to protect you in every way and will stop any attempts to enter into unauthorised intimacy with you in order to snatch pieces of resources from your life space.

It's not yourself or the relationship as such that needs to be protected, but the spiritual choice. The choice to stay in intimacy, to go that way, to forgive and let people go, to let them be in intimacy with themselves, with their horrible decisions and strategies. You have to protect everything within yourself.

All relationships where you don't have intimacy, especially relationships with your children, are karmic relationships due to mutual deficits and needs. And very often, if we conceive a child without spiritual awareness, but just by having sex, a certain level of soul comes as well. And, if you have had a 'routine conception', then you have invited a soul into your life, before which you have great karmic debts, and you have to cover the deficits of that soul.

You should not be upset that there is no special intimacy, you just need to work on this relationship and help the child to develop, that is to say, throw all your energy into helping them to form an intimacy with themselves. Cover their needs and deficits first, and then see if this relationship is capable of moving to the next stage of development.

Sometimes child–parent relationships don't transition into intimacy. It is important for your soul to evolve this energy, this form of relationship. You may still have a relationship with your child, in which they have needs, and you teach them how to meet these needs properly, ecologically. Accordingly, you set yourself up to foster intimacy of the child with themselves as much as possible—that is your parental duty.

If you accomplish this, consider yourself a genius parent, because it is a great art to raise children who are in intimacy with themselves. And if it is not there between you, look for it elsewhere, and leave your family alone, because that is not the place where such high spiritual tasks are solved.

Intimacy Meditation

Concentrate on your breath. Feel that you are sitting in a comfortable, quiet environment. Close your eyes and begin to dive your attention into the inner space, your inner psychological territory. Feel your breath become conscious and go down to your lower abdomen, as if you are breathing with your belly and your whole body. Enter into a state of peace and tranquillity.

Feel yourself fully present here and now. Give yourself this time of relaxation, this time when you are accumulating energy and strength, doing the very important work of creating a space of intimacy with yourself.

Feel this special state of intimacy with yourself, when the most important being for you on Earth is you, when the most important relationship is a relationship with yourself. Feel how you accept yourself completely as you are, how important this closeness with yourself is to you, how much you miss yourself.

Say in your mind: "I accept myself fully and completely as I am. I give space within myself to all my states, all my experiences, all my feelings, thoughts, events, worries, fears, conjectures, joys."

Feel now how your heart is embraced by a state of peace and a comprehensive state of unity with yourself, and give space within yourself to all the events of your life. Feel what a relief your soul feels when you give yourself this intimacy when you give yourself time to simply contemplate yourself from within, and to see and accept all that is in you, and to give everything a place in your soul, in your heart, in your consciousness.

Now give the right of intimacy with yourself to everyone you know who is important and dear to you.

Say within yourself: "I acknowledge the right to intimacy with me of my loved ones and realise how important it is to them. I guard my loved one's sacred space of intimacy. I perceive their space of intimacy with me as a sacred temple with all the freedoms that my kindred person, my kindred people, need. I feel how my significant other needs these freedoms, and I want to help my significant other become more and more free and more intimate with themselves."

Feel how you thereby give more freedom to yourself and more intimacy, for what you give away, you always get back. Feel how the states of intimacy and freedom are interconnected within you, and answer yourself the question of what freedom you lack and in what you limit yourself.

Expand the boundaries of your freedom within your heart and soul now; ask yourself what you dream of and where you delude yourself about your freedom, how your desire for intimacy widens with the growth of your territory of freedom. Feel the special energy of intimacy as you live in a state of freedom.

Give yourself now the gift of the union in your soul of these two divine awesome energies—the energy of being in intimacy and the energy of being free. Feel the same experience within your partner as you bless them, whether it's your child, or a loved one in the family, or your parents, or your friend. Whoever it is, feel how your shared space has changed since you both chose intimacy and freedom.

What has changed in the quality of states, in the quality of vibrations? What has changed in the way you feel about the world? What needs and deficits have closed on their own, automatically? Simply begin to let go of all deficits and all needs that become irrelevant if you move into a state of freedom and intimacy.

What do you stop worrying about; what do you stop fearing? What are you giving up as your past? What life scenarios are you letting go of? Imagine that they're just going over the horizon, far, far away. You let them go easily and simply.

And now feel how out of a space of freedom and intimacy, you become one with the whole world. Feel your intimacy to the designs of God, of all the people, of all the cities in which you live, feel how one you are with the whole world. Experience the state of intimacy with our planet, let it into your heart, feel that it is within you and you are within it.

Now you can think of any people with whom you've had difficult relationships and say to them mentally: "I give you every kind of freedom within me that I can give. I acknowledge your intimacy with myself, and I acknowledge whatever form of intimacy that has arisen between us, whatever it may be. And in that intimacy, I also give freedom to myself and to all living beings."

Incorporate this quality of freedom and intimacy into every relationship that is meaningful to you right now. Feel your heart, your consciousness, your perception change. You may get answers to questions about what freedom you fear or have been afraid of, what you are scared of, and how allowing yourself to be free now dissolves those fears.

How intimacy with yourself becomes a special quality that settles forever in your heart, becomes a higher value, a higher criterion, a higher bar.

Now try to imagine yourself twenty years from now and try to see what kind of intimacy you want to experience at that age, with whom or with what. And, how close you will really be to yourself, what your space of intimacy will be in twenty years...just observe all the things you will see and feel.

What will be your freedom, what will be your intimacy, and what will both of these energies fill you with? What do you enjoy most about this kind of life of true intimacy and freedom, what is truly valuable, what is truly precious? What is the revelation of such a life, what is its gift? And, how do you see the partnership with your closest people twenty years from now?

What kind of relationship is it, what is it based on, how is it built? What are you contributing to that relationship? What rewards do you get for sincerely serving the relationship from a state of intimacy?

Life itself becomes the greatest gift when your heart and soul serve the freedoms of intimacy, the freedoms of fulfilment. Now look at yourself, what you will be like if you devote twenty years of your life exclusively to the synthesis and quality of special intimacy in a state of intelligent freedom. What fears will you let go of that will never come back to you?

What doubts will you overcome and become a different person? And, why is it so important to you? What kind of family will you have and what will that family be for you? What will you be truly inspired by? See how your sense of deficit space will change dramatically, what place deficits will occupy in your life, and how you will learn to deal with them. What strengths and resources do you gain when you live a life of abundance on all levels?

Look within yourself. How has your heart space changed, how has your well-being, your mood, and even your plans for today changed? What values do you now want to preach within yourself, and what do they mean to you?

And gradually go back.

I hope you were able to have a deep, interesting, qualitative experience.

What has become important to you? What have you realised? What does loyalty to yourself mean to you? What do your boundaries of freedom mean to you? What does the state of intimacy with yourself, with the world, with other people mean to you? If you have come to a state of special peace and tranquillity, then you have meditated correctly, you have succeeded.

Now write down what kinds of freedom are important to you. We talked about three forms of freedom that are very important to each person.

Freedom of information, of learning, of knowledge, of changing one's consciousness as such.

Freedom of movement, freedom to discover new territories, new boundaries in life. The freedom to stay alone also belongs to freedom of movement. If you have a desire to be alone, this is a very important form of freedom for you, without which there is no true intimacy with yourself.

Freedom of communication, the ability to give yourself those people, to the extent that they are valuable and important to you.

Designate these forms of freedom that you see in front of you now as something that you need to go towards, something that you want to achieve, that you aspire to.

And finally, define for yourself your new views on intimacy: where, how, and why you would like to perform a healing of intimacy. What is intimacy healing for you—intimacy healing with your soul, intimacy healing with your family or your partner? Why is it important to you; how do you see yourself going forward; how will you heal intimacy—with freedom, with attention, with forgiveness? How will you bring additional intimacy into your heart, into your soul?

Maybe in the way that Paul the Apostle did and spoke about it, who united both intimacy and love and forgiveness and freedom and the best thing in the universe, God.

...If I speak in the tongues a of men or of angels, but do not have love, I am only a resounding gong or a clanging cymbal.

If I have the gift of prophecy and can fathom all mysteries and all knowledge, and if I have a faith that can move mountains, but do not have love, I am nothing.

If I give all I possess to the poor and give over my body to hardship that I may boast, but do not have love, I gain nothing.

Love is patient, love is kind. It does not envy, it does not boast, it is not proud.

It does not dishonour others, it is not self-seeking, it is not easily angered, it keeps no record of wrongs.

Love does not delight in evil but rejoices with the truth. It always protects, always trusts, always hopes, always perseveres.

Love never fails. But where there are prophecies, they will cease; where there are tongues, they will be stilled; where there is knowledge, it will pass away.

For we know in part and we prophesy in part, but when completeness comes, what is in part disappears.

When I was a child, I talked like a child, I thought like a child, I reasoned like a child. When I became a man, I put the ways of childhood behind me.

For now we see only a reflection as in a mirror; then we shall see face to face.

Now I know in part; then I shall know fully, even as I am fully known...

Ya Ali
(getting closer to the Creator)

In Conclusion

In the first quarter of the twenty-first century, we have passed psychologically from the Middle Ages into a not very long period of Renaissance of the spirit, which will last about seventy years and end by the end of our century.

The Renaissance marks the flourishing of the individual creative spirit in people through connection with their divine nature. The only thing that makes this possible is the divine energy of love, without which no evolution of the soul is possible.

Sensing this change, mankind is searching more than ever for ways to achieve harmony in couples' relationships. Science is creating new methods of analysing compatibility. Spiritual teachers are helping us through our states of unconsciousness. Aggravated aggressive conflicts suggest that without the value of love, our civilisation simply has no future in any dimension.

Formulas for finding unity, in any case, begin with the intimate connection people have with one another, which is one of the key tasks of the evolution of our era of change. And what that connection will be is up to each person, based on the exercise of his or her free will.

We wish you that this path will include Wisdom, Knowledge, and the highest form of pure Divine love.